Originally published in 1905 by
Archibald Constable & Co. Ltd., London

This edition portions © 2013 by Bunkasha International Corporation
— second edition —
Foreword by Alex Bennett

ISBN 978-4-907009-04-5

For further information on this and other martial arts books please visit us at:

www.kendo-world.com

F.J. NORMAN'S
THE FIGHTING MAN
OF JAPAN

F.J. NORMAN'S THE FIGHTING MAN OF JAPAN

Sketching the Life and Career of F.J. Norman – Western Kendo Pioneer –

By Alex Bennett[1]

Francis James Norman (1855-1926) was a Western pioneer of the modern Japanese martial arts who was one of the first to introduce *kenjutsu* (*kendo*) to audiences outside Japan. Apart from writing about the martial culture of Japan, his actual skill in *kenjutsu* earned him considerable respect from Japanese. Upon a chance discovery of his 1905 book *The Fighting Man of Japan: The Training and Exercises of the Samurai* (Archibald Constable & Co. London, 1905), I was curious to find out more about the man and his career. A rare and valuable little volume, it remained almost completely unknown for an entire century. The author became a virtual recluse after the book's publication, even though it is one of the first comprehensive English language treatises

1 An earlier version of this article, "The FJ Norman Saga", was published in *Kendo World* Volume 3. 3, KW Publications, 2006

III

on *kenjutsu* and other traditional Japanese martial arts, and life at the prestigious Imperial Naval College at Etajima, where he served as an English teacher.

The book consists of 4 chapters:

1. Commencement of Japanese Military History
2. The Education of the Japanese Military and Naval Officers etc.
3. "Kenjutsu", or Japanese Fencing
4. Japanese Wrestling- Sumo and Jujutsu

He penned the book at the request of the "Japanese School of Ju-Jitsu" in London. Although his expertise was mainly in *kenjutsu*, they hoped the book would assist in the propagation of *jujutsu* in Great Britain.

Norman offers some marvellous insights into Japanese society in the late Meiji period (1868-1912), and more specifically, he provides modern readers with a first-hand record of what *kenjutsu* was like at the end of the nineteenth century. Although he also studied *jujutsu*, *kenjutsu* was his speciality, and his skill in the traditional art seems to have been highly respected by his contemporaries. For example, Ernest John Harrison (1873-1961), a *judo* practitioner who spent twenty years in Japan as a journalist from 1897, towards the end of Norman's sojourn, had the following words of praise for Norman's exploits.

> Perhaps the only foreigner who ever took up *kenjutsu* seriously is Mr. F.J. Norman, late of the Indian Army, a cavalry officer, and expert in both rapier and sabre play. Norman was for some years engaged as a teacher at the Etajima Naval College, and while there devoted his attention to the Japanese style to such good purpose that he speedily won an enviable reputation among the Japanese, and engaged in many a hard-fought encounter. Some few other foreigners have practised, and doubtless do practice kenjutsu for the sake of exercise, but I am not aware that any one of them has won distinction in Japanese eyes. (E.J. Harrison, *The Fighting Spirit of Japan*, T. Fisher Unwin, 1913, p. 103)

Indeed, Norman himself suggests that he was probably the first

Western exponent of *kenjutsu* to study it in depth, eventually reaching a highly respectable level of proficiency.

> While acting in that country as an instructor in some of the leading colleges, both military and civilian, the author has had what are, perhaps, unrivalled opportunities of making a thorough and systematic study of the two "noble sciences" of *kenjutsu* and *jujutsu*. The author is, so far as he is aware, the first Occidental who has gone at all deeply into these two branches of Japanese education.

There were a small number of Westerners who trained under notable swordsmen such as Sakakibara Kenkichi (1830–1894), but arguably none to the extent that Norman did. His attraction to what must have seemed a bizarre looking activity from the perspective of anyone versed in Western fencing apparently lay in the educational and recreational potential which he saw in the Japanese martial arts. He states in his introduction that the benefit he derived from his pursuit in these arts led him to the conviction that many advantages might be gained even to his native country "from the introduction of exercises so admirably calculated to improve the physique and also the morale of its youth and manhood."

He observed that the favourite games of "young England", probably being cricket, rugby and football, were necessarily restricted in practice to the few, meaning the upper classes. This predicament arose through the expensive nature of equipment, the time-expenditure involved, and the cost of preparing the grounds for play. He pointed out that the majority of people could only enjoy sporting activity as spectators. "Lookers on, it is said, see most of the game; but neither morale nor physique are thereby greatly benefited, and looking on is apt to degenerate into a dull pastime unless relieved by betting." Norman contended that the Japanese martial arts, namely *kenjutsu* and *jujutsu*, required no such costly equipment, and are exercises in which "all can participate, without risk or danger to life, purse, or limb, but with great benefit both to body and spirit."

Interestingly, even though Norman saw the great educational benefits to be gained in training in *kenjutsu* and *jujutsu*, he was by no means convinced that the spirit behind these vestiges of Japanese martial culture were in any way superior to the spirit of "sportsmanship" from his own British culture. He actually criticises the then much heralded spirit of *bushido* and the writings about it that were starting to flourish at the beginning of the twentieth century. By the time his book was published, the

Japanese had just defeated the Russians in the Russo-Japanese War (1904-1905). This seemingly miraculous victory over one of the world's superpowers was considered by the Japanese as an embodiment of "the glory of Meiji Japan", and the "Japanese spirit." To many observers, both Japanese and foreign, this was also representative of the spirit of *bushido* as glorified in the English writings of Nitobe Inazo, Uchimura Kanzo, and so on.

Norman, however, is quick to point out that, as opposed to the respect shown to the weak by the European knight, the Japanese maxim was "all is fair in love and war", and the samurai had a propensity to act in the most dishonourable fashion, committing "evil acts" to achieve a desired goal. He warns, "It may be said, indeed of our Japanese allies that they are firmly convinced that the end justifies the means." In regards to *kenjutsu*, perhaps reminiscing on some painful personal experiences during training, he makes the observation that "Japanese swordsmen resort to certain methods which are highly reprehensible from our point of view. Such a thing as giving another man a chance never appears to enter their heads; and so, should a fencer lose his *shinai* [bamboo practice sword], or fail in any way, his adversary immediately takes advantage of this to push home his attack with all the greater vigour."

But, what of the man himself? Apart from his training experiences in Japan, there is little autobiographical information is forthcoming in his book. There is no information about his place of birth, military career, and reasons for travelling to Japan. Even his full name is not to be found. With little to go on apart from a small clue at the beginning of his book where he stated that he was in the "14th Hussars", I conducted an investigation to find out more about the author. A search of the British Army Lists and War Office records found Norman's service record, "WO 76/549", the records of services of officers of the 14th Hussars stationed at Secunderabad, Madras, from 1826 to 1891. In this record I discovered that his full name was Francis James Norman, and that he was gazetted a lieutenant in the 14th Hussars on December 10, 1881, after serving in the ranks for 5 years and 187 days. The entry gives his date of birth as March 6, 1855, which is slightly at variance with the date quoted on his service record. No war service is indicated at the date of publication, and he probably did not see action as there is no reference to it on his service record either.

The record WO 76 is more revealing, but not as much as is the case with other officers. This is probably because there was less to reveal, his regimental career having been comparatively short. According to this service record, he was born on February 23, 1855 at Mooltan in the Punjab (then in British India, now spelt Multan and in Pakistan). Apparently he could speak "Hindustani" (Urdu). His service in the ranks, was spent entirely in the 11th Hussars, and began on June 6, 1876, with the rank of private, finishing on December 9, 1881, as a sergeant, after which he received his commission in the 14th Hussars. From December 1877 to January 1882 he was based in Great Britain, thereafter serving in the East Indies until February 4, 1887, the day he left the regiment.

His record is annotated "Superseded 4 Feb, 87", but there is no information as to the manner of his departure (transfer, resignation, dismissal etc.) Under the column headed "Date of Half Pay" the abbreviation "appt." appears. This could mean that he received another "appointment" so that half pay was inapplicable. He was not married at the time as the word "Single" appears very faintly in the space left for "Married or Single".

As his service record stops here, it suggests that this is the time he made passage to Japan. In fact within the text of his book he states "The summer of 1888 found me established in Tokyo..." A search of the "Japan Directory", a comprehensive list of foreigners residing in Japan during the Meiji Period, shows his name for the first time in the 1889 edition. For the first three years he resided in the Kanto region (around Tokyo) and taught (presumably English) at the prestigious First Higher Middle School in Tokyo. From 1894, he is listed as living at "Etajima in Hiroshima", the home of the Imperial Naval College. His name disappears from the records after 1899.

As his book was published in London in 1905, it is safe to assume that he had left Japan and moved back there around this time, if not a little earlier. He participated in a public demonstration of *kenjutsu* and *jujutsu* which was reported in *The Times* on October 19, 1905.

> Ken-jitsu, sword play with the Japanese two-handed sword, was illustrated by Mr. Norman and Mr. Miyake to the great amusement of the spectators—for etiquette seems to ordain that the Japanese swordsman should bark like a dog over the attack, and crow like a cock when he gets a blow home. Mr. Norman also tried a bout with Sergeant-Major Betts, who used a single-stick against his sword, with the result that the sergeant-major was metaphorically bisected once or twice and that Mr. Norman got some shrewd blows. But the impression produced was that Ken-jitsu is not really or nearly so important an exercise as Ju-jitsu.

The Times on October 19, 1905

After this, however, I was unable to locate any further information on his activities. Fortunately, just when all avenues of investigation seemed exhausted, I received a promising lead from Professor James Baxter, a colleague at the International Research Centre for Japanese Studies. He discovered a reference to another book written by Norman that was published in Calcutta in 1916. The book titled *Notes and a Report on the Kazusa System of Deep Boring for Water* (Thacker, Spink & Co.) is an extremely rare booklet, but I managed to locate the only known copy in Japan in the Kazusa Museum in Chiba Prefecture. Kazusa was the former name for modern day Chiba. The museum kindly agreed to let me analyse the content.

What I had hoped to confirm was that the book was actually written and published in Calcutta in 1916. This would verify that he was alive at least up to 1916, and that he probably resided in India after leaving England. It would then be a simple exercise to search the colonial birth and death records for India to establish exact year of death, and cause. I had already checked the most likely records in Great Britain, but could find not any reference of him remaining there after 1905. Close inspection of the book revealed that it had actually been written in 1902, and was penned in a place called Inage, in Japan. By pure coincidence, I

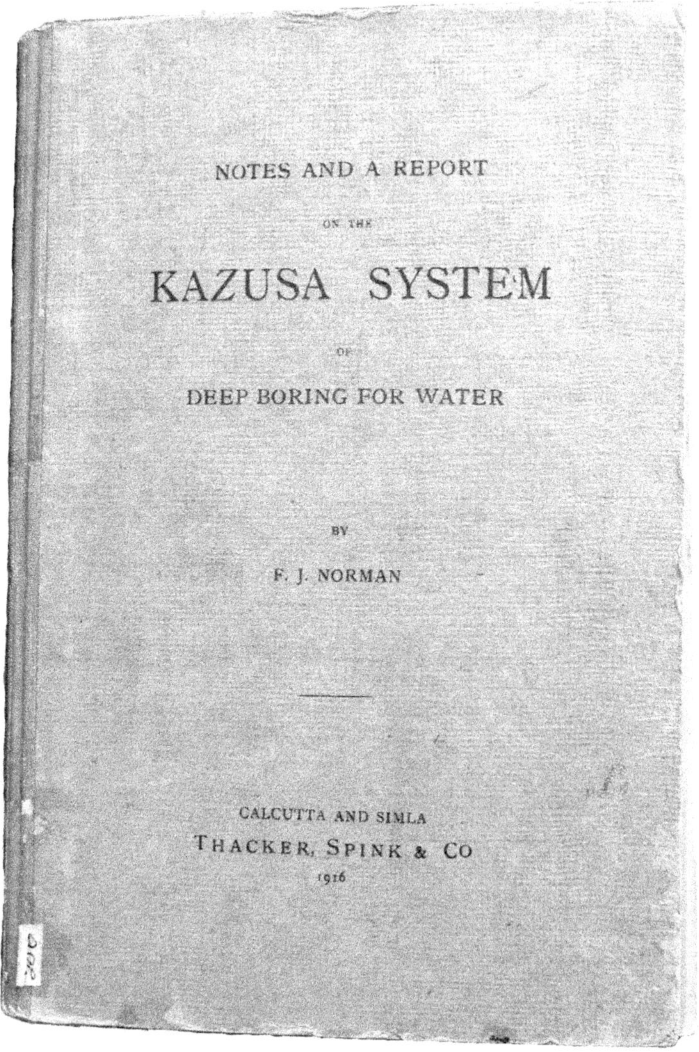

NOTES AND A REPORT

ON THE

KAZUSA SYSTEM

OF

DEEP BORING FOR WATER

BY

F. J. NORMAN

CALCUTTA AND SIMLA

THACKER, SPINK & CO

1916

XIII

The Kazusa well boring system

started my kendo career at Inage Municipal High School as an exchange student in 1987! It seems that the book was reprinted in 1916 due to popular demand, but ultimately provided no clue as to where F.J. Norman may have ended up.

PUBLISHERS' NOTE.

THE Second Edition of this very useful book was published in 1902. There has been a steady demand for it ever since and the impression has become exhausted. The Publishers feel that no apology is necessary for the present reprint which, as far as they know, is the only detailed description of the Kazusa System of Well Boring.

After republishing *The Fighting Man of Japan* through Kendo World Publications in 2003, and including a plea to readers for any more information about his whereabouts subsequent to the last reference I could find dated October 1905, I received an e-mail from Mrs. Mary Bassendine in England. Evidently, F.J. Norman was her grandfather, and she wondered if she could "purchase a few copies of the republication..." A box of books was dispatched forthwith, along with a myriad of questions to find out what happened to him after he went to England in the early 1900s. The following reply came from Mrs. Bassendine:

> My grandmother used to have a sepia photo of my grandfather in Army uniform on her mantle piece and my father took this to the India Office in London where they identified the regiment he belonged to and looked up his records. My father was writing a book about another famous Norman family member, Field Marshal Henry Wylie Norman, at the time. He also had a very interesting life in the service of the Indian Army. We were sad that my father did not take more interest in finding out more about his father, but perhaps this was too painful for him, as his father died when he was at such a critical age. Unfortunately he [FJN] died in 1926 when my father was only 16, leaving my grandmother to bring up the three boys, Frank, Bill and Howard on her own. My father was the second son, born in 1910. His brother Frank was two years older. My grandmother was very much younger than him. He must have been in his fifties and her in her twenties when they married. I do not know the date of their marriage, but it must have been between 1905 and 1907. All

three sons, including my father, Bill, are now dead, but my cousins, my brothers and sister have regular Norman celebrations. All of us have bits and pieces of information about our grandfather, but nobody has brought this all together. We have one lovely photograph of him looking into a mirror and writing in Japanese script. A Japanese friend told me that he was writing "Happy New Year". She was surprised that he could write so well with a brush.

I had an opportunity to visit the Bassendine family near Seven Oaks just outside London. I met members of the Norman clan and was able to discuss the family's history. It became apparent that he was a man of great mystery, even to his own family. To quote Mrs. Bassendine again,

There are a number of stories about F.J. Norman which we are not sure of. My father told us that he left the Indian Army to be tutor to a Maharaja, that he was a War Correspondent for the Daily Telegraph and that there was some sort of family rift, surrounding his marriage. My grandmother was a doctor's daughter, and thought to be 'beneath him socially', so the family cut him off. I do not know whether

F.J. Norman's three sons

F.J. Norman's wife

XIX

F.J. Norman brushing "Happy New Year"

GIVEN AT THE GENERAL REGISTER OFFICE

Application Number G250701

Marriage solemnized at The Register Office in the District of Kensington in the County of London

No.	When Married	Name and Surname	Age	Condition	Rank or Profession	Residence at the time of Marriage	Father's Name and Surname	Rank or Profession of Father
97	Fourteenth February 1908	Francis James Norman	52	Bachelor	Gentleman	23 Addison Road Bayswater	Francis Booth Norman deceased	Officer in H.M.S.
		Margaret Lily John Smith	22	Spinster	—	13 th place Bayswater	George Smith	Watering Inspector

Married in the Register Office according to the Rites and Ceremonies of the _____, by Licence after by me,

This Marriage was solemnized between us,	{	F.J. Norman	in the Presence of us,	{	A.H. Linton Richard J. Martin

CERTIFIED to be a true copy of an entry in the certified copy of a register of Marriages in the Registration District of Kensington

Given at the General Register Office, under the Seal of the said Office, the 25th day of April 2004

MXB 603724

F.J. Norman's marriage certificate

XXI

the reason for this is true, but there was no contact between my grandmother and his family, even when she was widowed so young with three boys. We understand that he had an older brother, Arthur, who went to Australia.

Apparently, being the daughter of a physician made her socially inferior. His wife being 30 years his junior, however, must surely have made him the target of unspoken envy for many.

F.J. Norman's descendants

From my father [FJN's second son] I know that as children they originally lived in Paddington, London. My father was a mischievous choirboy at St James church there. My grandfather [FJN] went to the First World War and was gassed in the trenches. He returned home to convalesce in Brighton and the family moved there, living in Kemp Town. The boys attended Brighton College. He died in an army nursing home and he is buried in a cemetery there. We did some research and found the plot where he is buried. Unfortunately the grave is unmarked. Having discovered this, we tried to persuade the family to contribute to a headstone, but did not succeed in this.

When Mrs. Bassendine's father went to the India Office, he discovered that Norman had left the Army "without leave". This might have explained the family's hostile attitudes towards him. Sir Francis Booth Norman (1830-1901) was a lieutenant-general and a highly decorated military man, and his older brother Sir Henry Wylie Norman (1826-1904) was a field marshal, the highest rank in the British Army. "Presumably they would have been dismayed at their young nephew behaving in this way. It upset my father rather, but to us, it made him a more interesting, more courageous person, who was prepared to go against the code of the time."

For reasons which nobody now knows, he decided to go to the front in the First World War. He would have been in nearly 60 years of age by then, which makes his decision surprising to say the least. It seems he was a victim of poisonous gas in the trenches, and he was forced to return to England to spend the rest of his days in a nursing home in Brighton. Why would he want to go to war at his age? What did he hope achieve? Was it an attempt to retrieve some respect in family circles? Whatever the case, his wounds distanced him from his direct family also; with a young wife and three young sons, he had no means to provide for them.

Together with the Bassendine family, I visited Brighton to search for the remnants of the nursing home, and also find his unmarked grave. We had a basic idea of where we should be looking, but it was a difficult task pinpointing the exact locations. We visited a number of cemeteries in Brighton to look for his grave site, finally discovering where he was laid to rest at the Brighton & Preston Cemetery in plot Q99, with no surviving headstone. Detailed records kept by the cemetery office enabled us to pinpoint the actual burial site. We were also able to access the city's "Births, Deaths and Marriages Registry". We were sent a copy of his death

F.J. Norman's grave

certificate the very next day, which confirmed the exact day of his death and occupation.

We also explored the Marine Parade and Arundel Street area to look for the nursing home. We had an address of where his wife and children lived when he was in the nursing home, but the street no longer existed. We discovered what we thought could have been the nursing home, but it proved difficult to verify, even after a trip to the local history and records office which stores

F.J. NORMAN'S THE FIGHTING MAN OF JAPAN

HC 919919

CERTIFIED COPY of an ENTRY OF DEATH
Pursuant to the Births and Deaths Registration Act 1953

Registration District Brighton

1926. Death in the Sub-district of East Brighton in the County of Brighton

No.	When and where died	Name and surname	Sex	Age	Occupation	Cause of death	Signature, description, and residence of informant	When registered	Signature of registrar
481	Third June 1926 Red Cross Hospital Marine Parade V.D.	Francis James Norman	Male	71 years	9 5 Arundel Street Brighton V.D. Author and Journalist	1 Bronchitis and Emphysema with myocarditis 8 years bo pm. Certified by John Aurden M.B.	Wm. N Norman Brother The Holt June 1926 Eynsham Oxford	Twentieth June 1920	J. Webb

Certified to be a true copy of an entry in a register in my custody.

_____ Superintendent Registrar

20. 11. 2004   Date

CAUTION: THERE ARE OFFENCES RELATING TO FALSIFYING OR ALTERING A CERTIFICATE AND USING OR POSSESSING A FALSE CERTIFICATE. ©CROWN COPYRIGHT

WARNING: A CERTIFICATE IS NOT EVIDENCE OF IDENTITY.

XXVI

thousands of registers and old newspapers from the region. We did find some old school newspaper articles with reference to Norman's sons and their athletic prowess in the boxing ring at Brighton College, but nothing related directly to their father.

Evidently, Norman was the proverbial 'black sheep' of a highly distinguished family, and his antics alienated him from his illustrious relatives. First, he left the army without leave, and ventured to Japan where he taught at a number of prestigious colleges. He also used this opportunity to 'go native' as it were, and undertook the study of *kenjutsu* and other aspects of Japanese culture. He recorded his experiences in a way which makes for fascinating reading. After leaving Japan and returning to England sometime after 1902, he married a woman whom his family did not approve of.

I suspect that this is as much as we will get to know the man with any concrete certainty, and anything else we will be no more than conjecture. His observations on the martial arts and other aspects of Japanese culture which he recorded over a century ago were astute. He was a gifted observer, with a clearly rebellious streak in his nature. His tendency to go against protocols in an extremely class-conscious British society may not have earned him the respect of some of his family members, but it enabled him to see and report things in a way that was impervious to cultural and social restraints. For this, he has left us a small but valuable legacy of information, and deserves our gratitude and respect. I hope that the republication of this volume will serve as a tribute to this unsung Western pioneer of the Japanese martial arts. I only wish I could have met him in person as I have so many more questions to ask...

Date	Event
1855 [Feb. 23]	Born Mooltan, Punjab, British India (now Multan, Pakistan), confirmed
1855 [March 6]	Alternative date of birth
1874	Application for a Queen's India cadet-ship made by his father, but later withdrawn in favour of a brother
1876 [June 6]	Starts career in 11th Hussars as private
1877 [December]	Travels to England
1881 [December 9]	Finishes in 11th Hussars as sergeant
1881 [December 10]	Joins 14th Hussars (stationed in Secunderabad, Madras) as lieutenant
1882 [January]	Leaves for the 'East Indies'
1886 [October 30]	14th Hussars leave Bombay for Shorncliffe, Kent on the troopship Serapis
[December 21]	The Times announces that FJN is superseded for absence without leave, and FJN disappears from the subsequent army list of Jan-Mar 1887

Date	Event
1887 [February 4]	Service record of this date is marked 'Superseded 4 Feb 87'. No half-pay, instead marked 'appt.' (contraction of appointment). Single
1888 [Summer]	Established in Tokyo, Japan
1889–1891	Living in the Kanto region. Teaching at the First High Middle School, Tokyo
1894–1899	Living at Etajima, Hiroshima (home of the Imperial Naval College)
1900	Observes Kasuza system of deep-boring for water. Possible solution to the Indian "Water Supply Question"
1902	Kasuza-well boring system book written in Inage
[December 21]	Publication of Notes and a Report on the Kazusa System for Deep Boring of Water (Thacker & Spink, Calcutta and Simla)
1905	Publication of The Fighting Man of Japan by Archibald Constable & Co., London
[October 18]	Gives informal lecture and demonstration of kenjutsu in London
1908 [February 14]	Married to Margaret Lily Gent in Kensington, London
19??	Birth of Frank
1910	Birth of William James Norman (Bill), later choirboy at St. James Paddington

Date	Event
19??	Birth of Valentine Howard Norman (Jim).
1916	Reprint of Kazusa book due to steady demand.
1917 [July 31]	Starts service in the 'New Armies' (later the Labour Corps) as a 2nd Lieutenant in the Chinese Labour Corps. (This contradicts Bill's indication that he was a linguist to Indian troops).
[August 18]	The Times mentions an F.J. Norman to be "temp. sec. lts. On" July 31 under the Gen. List. of the Infantry. Confirms above
1918	Entered for a "Silver War Badge" generally awarded on being injured and invalided out, presumably because of mustard gas exposure. However, this was cancelled as he was still in service as of 25-8-1918
1920 [May]	Ends service as temporary Lieutenant in the Chinese Labour Corps
1926 [June 3]	Died from a lung condition acquired 8 years earlier during WWI, at the Red Cross Hospital on Marine Parade, or Percival Terrace. Previous address: 5 or 3 Arundel Street. Occupation according to death certificate: "Author and Journalist"
1926 [June 8]	Buried at Brighton & Preston Cemetery in Q99, no surviving headstone. His brother, William Wylie Norman was the informant

THE FIGHTING MAN OF JAPAN

The Training and Exercises of the Samurai

by F. J. NORMAN

.. THE ..
JAPANESE SCHOOL
OF JU-JITSU.

Chief Instructors :
MR. MIYAKE AND MR. TANI.

Instructors :
MR. EIDA AND MR. KANAYA.

Assistant Instructors:
MESSRS. COLLINGRIDGE, McDONNELL
AND HOBDAY.

Instructor for Ladies :
MISS ROBERTS.

The School will be open for lessons from 9 a.m. to 10 p.m.

According to the hour of the day there will be two or three or four instructors at work.

The day is divided into lesson periods. Pupils who desire to do so may book in advance (at the School or by telephone) any particular period with any particular instructor.

M. ALLERDALE GRAINGER,
Secretary.

XXXII

THE FIGHTING

MAN OF JAPAN

A GROUP OF OFFICERS AND INSTRUCTORS AT THE IMPERIAL NAVAL COLLEGE, ETAJIMA, WITH THE AUTHOR AMONG THEM

XXXIV

THE FIGHTING MAN OF JAPAN

THE TRAINING AND EXERCISES OF THE SAMURAI

BY

F.J. NORMAN

LATE 11th AND 14th HUSSARS, LATE INSTRUCTOR IN GOVERNMENT COLLEGES OF
JAPAN - CIVIL AND MILITARY

WITH 32 ILLUSTRATIONS

XXXV

F.J. NORMAN'S THE FIGHTING MAN OF JAPAN

INTRODUCTION

THE author of the following brochure is an old soldier, who has been for many years resident in Japan. While acting in that country as an instructor in some of the leading colleges, both military and civilian, he has had what are, perhaps, unrivalled opportunities of mating a thorough and systematic study of the two "noble sciences" of *kenjutsu* and *jujutsu*. The author is, so far as he is aware, the first Occidental who has gone at all deeply into these two branches of Japanese education. The benefit he has derived from their pursuit has led him to the conviction that much advantage might accrue to his native country from the introduction of exercises so admirably calculated to improve the physique and also the morale of its youth and manhood. The favourite games of young England are necessarily restricted in practice to the few, owing to the expensive nature of the requisite appliances, the time-expenditure involved, and the cost of preparing the ground. The majority can enjoy them only in the role of spectators. Lookers on, it is said, see most of the game; but neither morale nor physique are thereby greatly benefited, and looking on is apt to degenerate into a dull pastime unless relieved by betting. No such costly appliances are required in connection with these Japanese exercises, in which all can participate, without risk or danger to life, purse, or limb, but with great benefit both to body and spirit. The following brief notes on the historical and practical side of *jujutsu* and *kenjutsu* make no pretence to being exhaustive, having been written rapidly with the express object of illustrating the general ideas and aims of the Japanese school of *jujutsu*. The author was unexpectedly summoned to assist the members of this school in giving a public demonstration of the art of *jujutsu*, in Great Britain. The time placed at his disposal for writing and issuing the following brochure was limited, and he claims the indulgence of its readers both on that score and in consideration of the fact that the ground he has covered has hitherto been practically untrodden.

CONTENTS

CHAPTER I

CHAPTER II

CHAPTER III

CHAPTER IV

XXXIX

F.J. NORMAN'S THE FIGHTING MAN OF JAPAN

LIST OF ILLUSTRATIONS

THE FIGHTING MAN OF JAPAN

CHAPTER I

Commencement of Japanese Military History

THERE would appear to be little doubt that the two main causes contributing toward the fighting and sea-faring instincts of the Japanese are--first of all, the strong strain of Malay blood that runs in their veins; and secondly, the favourable climatic conditions under which they have been bred and brought up. The Malay strain has given them evidently the necessary fire, bravery and dash for the calling of warriors; to the second or climatic cause they owe those physical qualifications without which the advantage of race is often of so little avail. As regards the peculiar discipline and loyalty for which the Japanese have now become so famous, these traits would appear to be the outcome of their Mongolian blood and teachings ; for if there is one thing for which Far Orientals are distinguished more than another it is that marked deference and loyalty to the wishes of a superior, without which discipline can rest on no sure basis. It was the introduction of Buddhism into the country, however, that gave the finishing touch to the character and ways of the Japanese warrior, as evolved in the shape of the samurai. Buddhistic teaching civilised and made a gentleman and a scholar of him, but never succeeded in spoiling him altogether for the rougher life of camps. For a century or so, it is true, the Japanese warrior appears to have been quite content with the newer ideas and teachings brought over from the mainland by the disciples of Shaka, yet, thoroughly and always manly at heart, he eventually got disgusted with their priestly rule; and so, taking the government of the country into his own hands again, he set to work applying his newly-gained knowledge to the feudalising of the national institutions.

With the introduction of feudalism into the country, the study of military arts and sciences spread apace among the "soldier gentry" of old Japan, and that is just what the *samurai* of old were. Japan has always turned to China for initiation and instruction upon the higher planes of thought and sentiment. And so it was to China that the *samurai* went in order to perfect themselves in their studies, but it was not long before they improved upon the teachings and methods of their models. And just why this should have been so may be gathered from the fact that while a Chinaman says : "One does not make a horse-shoe out of good iron, nor a soldier out of a good man," the Japanese say: *Hana wa sakura hito wa bushi*; or, "What the cherry is among flowers, so the *bushi* is among men." Or in other words -the cherry blossom being, in the estimation of the Japanese, the purest and noblest among flowers, so the *bushi*, or warrior, is the purest and noblest among men.

As a result of such high ideas, *bushido*, or "the way of the warrior," soon became, as it still is, a most important factor in the education, guidance and training of the Japanese soldier and official. But about this same *bushido* a great deal of nonsense has been written of late ; for, comparing it with the chivalry of the West, we find that while the European knight considered it his duty to respect women and the weakness and unpreparedness of a foe, the bushi, on the other hand, held to the maxim that "all is fair in love and war," and scrupled not to resort to devices of the most dishonourable kind in order to gain a desired object. And then, again, his sense of *giri*, or duty, never prevented a *bushi* from committing an evil act if such an act were only done in the service of his feudal lord. And much the same sort of thing held good even among the *samurai* women : as for instance when a mother sacrificed her younger children to save the life of her first-born, or a daughter consented to sell her chastity in order to pay the debts contracted by a dissipated father. All such, and many similar acts, were, and are still, allowable in Japan. It may be said, indeed, of our Japanese allies that they are firmly convinced that "the end justifies the means."

Until lately the *bushi* or *samurai* were easily distinguishable from the remainder of their fellow-countrymen, not less by their peculiar carriage of the body, begotten by the constant practice of martial exercises, than by the two swords stuck in those girdle sashes without which they never appeared in public. The longer of these two swords, the *katana*, was the *bushi's* main weapon of offence and defence, and the shorter, the *wakizashi*, or dirk, with a blade of from eight to twelve inches in length, was what they committed *hara-kiri* with.

[For an explanation of this see Chapter III.] Beside learning how to wield their swords aright all *bushi* underwent instruction in archery, the use of the halberd and lance, and in *jujutsu;* while many were, also, taught how to handle a boat, to swim, and to ride a horse. How to keep their weapons in order, bow to bear pain, heat and cold, starvation and thirst, how to put up with the fewest possible wants these are a few of the subjects of instruction included in the physical education of every true *bushi*. Along with his instruction in all these soldierly accomplishments every *bushi* received a scholastic and literary education, and in the case of many of them this was by no means of an inferior order. At first, as has already been noted, it was Buddhism and its teaching that attracted their allegiance ; but later on, as Chinese became the classical language of the country, the Confucian Classics, the "Four Books" and the "Five Canons" took the place of the *Sutras*, and so continued to do until the advent of European ideas and civilisation. With the arrival of Mendez Pinto, the Portuguese navigator and discoverer of Japan, in 1542, the Japanese first learnt the use of firearms and fortifications. But while they appear to have readily adopted the Western system of fortifications, they were decidedly chary in taking to the musket and why this was so may perhaps be explained by the fact that the harquebus of those days could have been little if at all superior to a well-strung bow, such as the Japanese seem to have had at that time. In range alone it may have been superior, but it is as likely as not that the Japanese bow possessed qualities superior in many other respects to that cumbersome and slow loading and firing shoulder piece. The precise character of the defensive works employed by the Japanese before 1542 is wrapped up in a good deal of mystery, though judging from the remarkable skill with which they now handle their wonderfully effective timbers, bamboos, and vines, and considering their Malay

PRINCE YAMATODAKE, ONE OF THE MOST FAMOUS
OF THE ANCIENT WARRIORS OF JAPAN

origin, it is most probable that stockades played a by no means unimportant part in them. I have been in many lands, but nowhere have I seen a country folk so clever in handling and rough-dressing timbers, and in making lashings out of creepers, as the Japanese, and certainly no creeper I have yet come across is so effective and generally useful for this last purpose as the wild wistaria of Japan. Freshly cut it is as pliable as a hempen cord, and when a lashing made of it has dried and hardened, then steel bands alone are superior to it.

It may, perhaps, be just as well to hark back here a little in order to show that the gift of military organisation is by no means a newly acquired art so far as the Japanese are concerned. For leaving out accounts dealing with the more apocryphal times, it is recorded of the aptly named Empress Jingo, that she organised and led an expedition against Korea in the year 200 A.D. But though the Emperor Sujin, 97-31 B.C., is said to have paid considerable attention to the subject of shipbuilding, yet there appears not to have been a sufficiency of sea-going craft in existence in Japan at that time for the warlike lady's purpose. Nothing daunted, she set to work building a perfect navy of transports ; just what they were like it is difficult to say, though there can be no doubt none of them were propelled by sail power.

Jingo Kogo's son Ojin, who is now worshipped in Japan as the "Spirit or God of War," is reported to have built a ship one hundred feet long. When completed it was tried at sea, and is said to "have been able to go through the water faster than a man could run on shore," and for this reason it was named *Karuno,* or the "Light One." When its timbers gave signs of giving out it was broken up, and with the exception of one piece, which was made into a *koto,* the so-called Japanese harp, the remainder was used as fuel for the production of sea-salt, the proceeds being applied to the building of new vessels. According to Japanese records there were at this time, upon one memorable occasion, no less than five hundred vessels collected in the harbour of Muko, but the tribute-bearer from Shiragi, one of the ancient divisions of Korea, that had been subdued by the dauntless Jingo, set them on fire-accidentally, it is said ; and in his anxiety to assist in repairing the mischief caused by his servant, the King of Shiragi sent over to Japan a number of clever naval architects. "From that time," say those same records, "the art of naval architecture became much improved and largely extended in Japan."

With the exception of a few short intervals of internal peace the Japanese appear to have passed their time, from the days of Jingo Kogo to the year 1275 A.D., in fighting among themselves, with the result that while families rose rapidly to power others sank no less rapidly. But in that year the Mongol Tartars, under Kublai Khan, having overthrown the reigning dynasty of China, and obtained the submission of all the surrounding states, commenced making haughty and unjust demands upon the Japanese. Rightly treating them with the contempt they deserved, the plucky islanders set to work preparing for the threatened invasion. The first attack made by the Mongols was upon Tsushima, but as this appears to have been repulsed without either side having incurred much loss, it may be taken for granted that it was nothing more than a feint in order to see of what stuff the defenders were made. Realising that he had to face a task of the most formidable character, Kublai Khan caused a number of warships to be built, of sizes and armaments unknown to the Japanese, and collecting an army of a hundred thousand fighting men he approached, in the fourth month of the year 1281, the castle town of Daizafu. Nothing daunted, the Japanese attacked him, and, helped by a mighty typhoon, which drove a number of the Mongol ships ashore, they literally wiped out the great armada. Of the whole invading force, it is said, that only three men returned to China to tell the tale. So great was the renown won by the Japanese as the result of this, that, with the exception of a few European and American marines, Japan has never since then been offended by the sight of a successful invader.

For the next two and a half centuries, until the arrival of Mendez Pinto, the Japanese busied themselves with fighting among themselves, each feudal lord in his fastness being a law unto himself. But the arrival of Hideyoshi upon the scene, that Napoleon of Japan as he has been called, resulted in the centralising of the authority of the State in a single person. The many years' civil war had, however, let loose upon the country a host of armed men, inured to fighting, and too proud to work, with the result that something had to be done, and so the sapient and masterful Hideyoshi decided upon an invasion of Korea, as a preliminary to an invasion of China. What his undertaking was like may be realised from the fact that over half a million of men took part in his Korean adventure, and that this immense force kept the field for over two years, during which time it so harassed and devastated the country that when Hideyoshi died, in 1592, his generals were only too glad of an excuse to return to Japan. Following this event a series of civil wars again broke out in the country, and were only brought to a conclusion at the great battle of Sekigahara, when

Iyeyasu, in 1603, having defeated all his foes, seized the reins of power. For over two and a half centuries the Tokugawas, as Iyeyasu's family name was, ruled Japan with a sufficiently strong hand to prevent any undue

A MEDIEVAL WARRIOR

disturbances breaking out. Among one of the many means they devised to ensure this was the forcing the daimyos, or feudal lords, to repair to their capital once a year, and to leave hostages there while absent from it.

F.J. NORMAN'S THE FIGHTING MAN OF JAPAN

The arrival of Europeans in the country gave an immense impetus to the art of shipbuilding in Japan ; but, true to their nature, the Japanese employed their newly gained knowledge more for other purposes than for peaceful pursuits, and their piratical raids upon Chinese shipping and along the China and Korean coasts developed to such an extent, that, to avoid a rupture with the governments of those two countries, the Shogun Iyemitsu, grandson of Iyeyasu, promulgated a law forbidding the building of ships above a certain tonnage. Had this law not been rigorously put into force, there is no saying what the Japanese empire might now have been. Siam, for instance, was for some years completely under the rule and guidance of certain Japanese adventurers, and a party of them even had the temerity to carry off into captivity the Dutch governor of Batavia. Some of them made their way to Madagascar and India, while others, joining hands with the Chinese pirates of Formosa, simply ruled that island and the waters about it. Just how these Vikings of the Far East were dreaded is amply exemplified by the numerous watch towers that still dot the whole of the North China coast, and also from the fact that despite the existence of many otherwise advantageous positions, all the coast towns and villages in Korea are-to use an Irishism --situated a few miles inland.

That the Spanish, Dutch, and other vessels which visited Japan from time to time were armed with cannon, may be taken for granted ; but, curiously enough, the Japanese do not appear to have taken to these weapons or ordnance so readily as might have been supposed. Hideyoshi's troops certainly did use both large and small guns in their expedition against the Koreans, but beyond mentioning the fact, none of the old records give satisfactory accounts of their so doing. We must not, however, lose sight of the fact that the Japanese have always been keen in-fighters, and that while all their old battles opened with discharges of arrows from both sides, this was invariably and quickly followed up by an advance of men skilled in the use of the spear, halberd and sword. Later on, toward the end of the seventeenth century, cannon were most effectually employed against the Christian rebels sheltering in the castle of Shimabara, but the guns in question were served (to their shame be it said) by Dutch gunners engaged by the Japanese authorities for this special purpose.

The arrival of the American squadron under Commodore Perry, in 1853, and its evolutions and gunnery practice, which that astute commander took very good care the Japanese should have every facility for seeing, opened the eyes of the Far Orient to the immense superiority of Occidental methods of warfare over their own ; and the result was that factories were at once established at Yedo and elsewhere for the manufacture of arms and ammunition on the Western plan. Some of the wealthier feudal lords, not content with the slow progress made by these local houses in turning out arms and munitions of warfare, secretly purchased a quantity from the foreign merchants then commencing to do business in Japan. Perceiving the trend of Japanese thought, and recognising that much profit might accrue to their respective compatriots by cultivating it, the foreign representatives commenced a series of negotiations which ended in the Shogun's government applying for and obtaining the services of military and naval instructors from abroad. The first military mission was entirely French ; but though it did excellent service, and undoubtedly laid the foundation for the present-day Japanese army, yet the revolution of 1868 and the disastrous result of the war of 1870 to the French colours induced the imperial authorities-who had by then taken the place of the Shogunate in the government of the empire-to engage German instructors in their place as the contracts of its various members lapsed. That these last did their duty there can be no doubt, but they achieved nothing like the success that has been so generally claimed for them, for there can be no disputing the fact that the Japanese army gained greater advantages from the swarm of officers sent to study in Europe than from any instructions it may ever have received from its imported instructors. And to say that the Japanese army tactics or organisation are copies of the German is to advance a claim that is absurd; for if they have not adopted more from the French, they certainly have adapted so much from other and various continental armies that the German share in it is but a fraction of the whole. Fighters and military organisers the Japanese have always been, as I have endeavoured to show ; and so all they had to learn, though that certainly was all-important, and yet not so difficult considering their military instincts, was how to employ to the best advantage the new arms and tactics then adopted by them. How quickly and how intelligently they picked up the knack of so doing may be gathered from the fact that when the rebellious Nagato forces invaded Buzen and Bungo, in 1866, the commander and officers of the gunboat Slaney, who witnessed the embarkation and disembarkation of the force, declared afterward that "it was

12

all executed in a manner that would have done credit to the best European troops."

Contrary to generally-accepted ideas upon the subject, to the Dutch, and not to the English, must be credited the first foreign attempt at training a Japanese naval force; though, at the same time, to the Portuguese and Spanish friars of the sixteenth century must be credited the first instructions given to the Far Easterners in the art of ship-building, as understood in the West, and in the science of navigation. What may justly be considered as of peculiar interest to all Englishmen is the fact that Will Adams, a fellow-countryman of theirs, who landed in Japan in April, 1600, was retained at the Court of Iyeyasu, the then Shogun, as a ship-builder, instructor as a sort of diplomatic agent when other English and Dutch traders began to arrive in the country. Considering how very much the Japanese are indebted to British instructions, help, and advice with regard to their naval matters, it is a curious coincidence, surely, that Will Adams's grave, at Hemi, is situated on the heights overlooking the present great naval yard of Yokosuka.

Not until two years after the abolition of feudalism, in 1869, did the Japanese think of organising a national navy, though just before this both the Shogun's government and the leading Daimyos possessed navies of their own. But these were composed of all sorts and conditions of vessels, from those of purely native style to others of European build and armament, though when of the latter they were seldom other than converted merchant ships and steamers. One or two possessed by the Shogun were, however, specially-built war vessels, and the first that was so built for him was the " Kaiyo-maru," a composite gun-boat of about one thousand tons burden, built in Holland. In 1858 the steam-yacht " Emperor "was presented to the Shogun by Lord Elgin, on behalf of the British Government," as a token of its friendship and goodwill " upon the signing of the first treaty between England and Japan. Ten years later the United

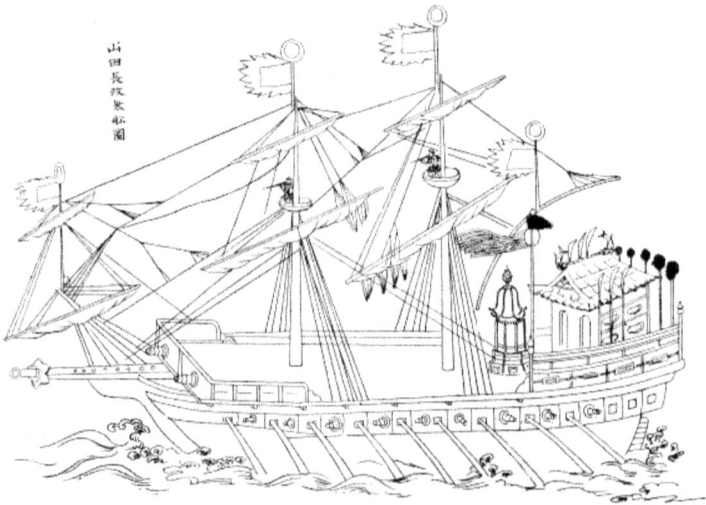

A VESSEL BUILT BY WILL ADAMS FOR THE JAPANESE
ABOUT 1600 A.D.

States Government handed over to the newly-constituted Imperial Government the iron-clad frigate "Stonewall Jack son" as a sort of sop for the scandalous treatment meted out to the then late Shogun, who had prepaid certain American contractors for a ship-of-war; when this vessel arrived in Japan the Japanese authorities, seeing it was not worth a quarter of the sum advanced; refused to take it over, and getting no redress from the United States representative in Japan, sent a mission to New York about the matter, with the aforegoing result. That there was some very unpleasant scandal behind the whole affair there can be no doubt, for it is difficult to understand how the United States Government was reimbursed the difference between the value of the two ships.

A FIGHT TO THE DEATH

CHAPTER II

The Education of Japanese Military and Naval Officers.

LEAVING out of consideration the little knowledge the Japanese picked up of navigation from their early Portuguese, Dutch, and English visitors during the sixteenth and seventeenth centuries, it was not until the early part of the late eighteen-sixties that a small naval mission was despatched by the Shogun's government to Holland, and it was the members of this mission, assisted by some Dutch officers and men, who brought the "Kaiyo-maru," already mentioned, to Japan. In 1867 the same Shogun's government applied for and obtained the services of a number of British officers and men as naval instructors. Unfortunately, however, this mission, under the leadership of Commander Tracey, R.N., had to be withdrawn by the British authorities because of the revolution which broke out a few months after its arrival in Japan, leading to the effectual overthrow of the Shogun's power. During the troublous times antecedent to and following the revolution, when no one knew exactly what was to follow, certain of the great Daimyos set to work organising their forces, naval as well as military. "One of them," as Professor Chamberlain says, " the Prince of Hizen, eager to possess a navy of his own, engaged Lieutenant Hawes, of the

Royal Marines, as gunnery instructor on board a vessel named the 'Ryujo Kan'; and this officer, who had an unusual talent for organisation, and who occupied himself, both on board the 'Ryujo Kan' and later on in other positions, with many matters besides gunnery and the training of marines, may be considered the real father of the Japanese navy."

When matters had somewhat quieted down, the new government, the Mikado's in contradistinction to the late Shogun's, applied to the British authorities for the services of a second naval mission, and as a result of this a party of officers and men under Commander Douglas, R.N., set out for and arrived in Japan in 1873. A naval college was formed at Tokyo, and after a certain number of picked officers and men had received the necessary instructions in gunnery, seamanship, &c., they were taken for a cruise to Australia and the islands between it and Japan. The work done was decidedly good, but needless to say some little friction arose at times between the instructors and the instructed, and more especially so with regard to matters of discipline. For it must here be explained that Japanese ideas of discipline at that time, though good enough in their way, were very different to what they now are. After putting in six years' service in Japan, this second naval mission returned to England, leaving behind, however, one or two officers and petty-officers as employees of the Japanese government.

In the early eighties the Naval College was removed to Etajima, in the Inland Sea, and an Academy, or Staff College, for officers, was established at Tokyo at the same time, while gunnery and torpedo schools were also organised. Candidature to the Naval College at Etajima is open to every male subject of the Mikado, with certain limitations as regards age, character and physique. Aspirants must be between fifteen and twenty years of age, and after furnishing the authorities with the requisite "character certificates" they are called upon to undergo a physical examination at the hands of a committee of naval surgeons, after which the entrance examinations take place. As the majority of such aspirants have been thoroughly coached at schools which make a speciality of such work the competition between them at the annual entrance examinations is invariably particularly keen. From 20 to 25 per cent fail to satisfy the demands of the doctors, and of the remainder only about 10 per cent succeed in passing the entrance examination. Having taken a part in many such examinations I can safely state that they are absolutely fairly conducted. The compulsory subjects are :-Under the head of mathematics - arithmetic, algebra, plane geometry, and plane trigonometry ; under the head of Japanese - literature and composition ; under the head of English - grammar, conversation, translation of Japanese into English and English into Japanese ; under the head of physics - chemistry, natural history and physical geography ; under the head of drawing and sketching - draughtsmanship both freehand and mechanical. There are besides a number of optional subjects, such as the Chinese, French, German, and Russian languages, marks awarded for which help the candidate - not so much to pass into the College as to secure a good position on the list of successful candidates. Once entered the College no cadet is allowed to resign under any pretext whatsoever ; but should the authorities find one of the cadets wanting either physically or in character and ability, that cadet is at once dismissed, and

AN ETAJIMA CADET

in my three years' experience of Etajima I only remember two of them being so dismissed from the College. Both these two were discharged for physical reasons; one because of failing eyesight, and the other because the surgeon in charge thought he detected signs of consumption in him. But, as a matter of fact, the surgeon was wrong, for young Beppu, a particularly nice lad, then went in for the army, and is now an artilleryman of great promise.

A better situation for a Naval College than Etajima it would indeed be difficult to find, for, in the first place, it is, as the termination to its name implies, an island, and though within easy reach of Kure and Hiroshima, yet so placed as to be well off the beaten track. So irregularly shaped is this island that Etajima Bay is well-nigh land-locked, and the College stands in ample grounds, with hills to the north, south, and east of it, and the waters of the bay to the west. The staff of officers and instructors is particularly large, the President being an admiral. In my days the course was a four-year one, but it has now been reduced to three years. During the first year four hours a week are given to gunnery, four to seamanship, one to engineering, six to English, five to physics, six to mathematics, making a total of twenty-six hours' study a week. Besides all this the cadet has at least an hour's drill a day, and receives instructions in *jujutsu*, fencing, gymnastics, rowing, &c. He will be required to get up within half-an-hour of sunrise, and will be served with breakfast at 7.30, lunch at noon, and dinner at 5.30 p.m. All work and studies are carried out in clean and neat white slop suits. Only on Sundays are the cadets allowed out of the College grounds, and even then for never more than three hours in the morning and three hours in the afternoon. Each class has its own club outside the College grounds, usually a farm house, where members of it may and do indulge in a little extra feeding, drinking and smoking, and, what is not allowed them whilst in the College grounds, in the reading of newspapers. The discipline kept is decidedly good, though to an average English youth it would be irksome beyond measure. Considering the advantages existing at Etajima it certainly is curious (and perhaps instructive) that none of the cadets ever think of going in for a little shooting or fishing ; but then the Japanese are not a sportingly inclined people. On one or two occasions I took a cadet or two out shooting or fishing with me, but it was easy to see that his heart was never in the sport; and this was the more remarkable, for such children of the officers, boys or girls, as I took out from time to time simply revelled in the delights of a day's shooting or fishing.

During the cadets' second year four hours a week are given to gunnery, three to seamanship, one to torpedo instruction, three to navigation, three to engineering, six to English, three to physics, and five to mathematics. During the third, or final, year, three hours a week are given to gunnery, four to seamanship, four to torpedo instruction, seven to navigation, one to engineering, six to English, and three to mechanics. Under the heading of seamanship are included instructions in the international rule of the road at sea, signalling, shipbuilding, provisioning and other kindred matters, and under the head of navigation the cadet has to study meteorology, surveying and the like. Beside all this the cadet will from time to time attend lectures upon international and civil law ; his naval history he gets up mostly while studying English. The training ship, launches, boats, the battery and the model rooms at Etajima are all thoroughly "up-to-date," and the instructions conveyed through their medium are practical and to the point.

Passing out of the College the cadet is promoted to midshipman, and is then, with a number of his class-mates, posted to one of the cruisers specially fitted up for the purpose. In my days the two cruisers that were so fitted up were the "Hiyei" and the " Kongo," but as the classes have now grown from sixty to two hundred three vessels are detailed for this purpose : the "Matsushima," the "Itsukushima" and the "Hashidate," sister ships of 4,200 tons. When all is ready these vessels start on a cruise lasting from six to eight months, and on returning to Japan the midshipmen are distributed among ships in commission. Two very good points to be here noted are that while a certain number of civilian instructors are attached to the College the greater part of the instructional work is carried out by naval officers, and that when a class has finished its three years' course a number of officers who have worked with them at the College accompany them on their finishing cruise.

At the end of a year or two the midshipman is promoted to a sub-lieutenancy, but only after having passed certain prescribed examinations. A Japanese naval sub-lieutenant is perhaps as hard worked an individual as exists, for not only has he to take his full share of watches and drills, but he is constantly being called upon to write reports and essays upon all sorts of matters, professional and otherwise ; but despite this last fact it is truly remarkable how little the Japanese naval officer is capable of discussing subjects other than purely professional ones.

EDUCATION OF MILITARY AND NAVAL OFFICERS

In two to four years' time the sub-lieutenant gets his lieutenancy, and if after a while he is reported upon favourably he is sent to the Naval Academy at Tokyo for a course in higher naval duties. Specially selected lieutenants go through a two years' course called "Koshu," and as this is done with a view to their after employment upon the staff, the subjects studied are strategy and tactics-- naval and military ; naval history ; fortifications ; law ; international law and diplomatic usages and history ; military and naval administration ; political economy; gunnery ; torpedo ; navigation ; ship building, and engineering. While undergoing this remarkably thorough and comprehensive course the officers arc sent from time to time to take part in various manoeuvres, to visit ships, forts, naval stations and factories when the same are being inspected by experts. Other lieutenants go through a course named "Otsushu," lasting one year, during the course of which they go in for the higher study of gunnery, torpedo and navigation duties. The idea governing this course is to turn out specialists in some one of the subjects named. Captains, commanders and senior lieutenants who have become a little rusty in certain subjects are allowed to attend a course called "Senka," but only so if it is considered they will truly benefit by so doing. Should an officer show special adaptability for a certain subject, and yet be lacking in others that might otherwise fit him for a staff appointment, he is put through a course called "Koshiuka." Besides these courses officers and men are constantly being put through practical courses at the schools of gunnery and torpedo at Yokosuka, and in addition to all this, special courses are formed for instruction in new weapons and scientific instruments for use with the same.

The non-executive branches of the Navy are particularly well provided for as regards instruction by special schools of their own. The Engineers' College at Yokosuka, and the rules regulating entrance to it, and the course of studies there, are based on lines similar to those that hold good with respect to the Naval College at Etajima. Yokosuka being a great dockyard and arsenal the College is therefore well situated for its purpose. Candidates for the Paymaster's Department are mainly recruited from graduates of the Imperial University, and after passing a course at the Paymaster's Training School at Tokyo they are first posted to ships in commission and later on to such as the exigencies of the service may demand. Petty officers and men, who are otherwise smart and useful but lacking in education, are also sent for a while to the Paymaster's Training School for educational purposes, as also are writers, cooks, etc.

While the officers of the Japanese Navy are recruited mainly from the best families in the empire, the men are recruited from its fisher folk, sea-faring and farming classes, and the result is that its personnel is of a very high order indeed. And though there is a good deal of heart-burning at times among a large section of the commissioned class, due to the all-predominating influence of the Satsuma element, yet on the other hand one never hears of those disgraceful bullyings and scenes among the seamen that are only too rife among the Mikado's soldiery. This is probably due to the fact that while the bluejackets are all recruited from much the same type of men, his soldiers are taken from all sections of

Japanese life, and so less cause for friction exists among the sailors than among the soldiers. That the Navy is the favourite branch of the service in Japan there can be no doubt, and the result is that a very goodly proportion of the men in it are volunteers and not (as in the Army) conscripts. A fearful lot of gush and nonsense has been written recently of the joy with which the Japanese conscripts join headquarters; but all who have lived among the people of the land know only too well that this joy is too often very much put on, and that while the majority of the bluejackets go back to civil life with some useful calling learnt while serving their time, the average soldier returns to it a spoilt and dissatisfied man.

The education of the Japanese military officer is as thorough as is the education of his comrade in the navy, and like him, too, he is mainly recruited from the better class *samurai* families. Unlike the naval officer, however, he has more than one way open to him for gaining a commission, at least during the first stages of his career. He may commence by graduating out of one of the many recognised Cadet Schools of the empire; or by graduating out of any Middle School, licensed and recognised by the government ; or if he can produce an educational certificate of the same value as that of a graduate's from a Middle School. In both these last two cases, however, an aspirant for a commission must obtain a nomination from the officer commanding the regiment or corps he is desirous of joining. Should he succeed in doing so, and is otherwise qualified, he then joins his regiment or corps as an "officer candidate," and as such is required to put in at least twelve months' service in the ranks in order to gain a complete and practical experience of all the duties of a soldier. Having done so to the entire satisfaction of his commanding officer he will next be drafted to the Military College, Tokyo, for an eighteen months' course in military arts and sciences, and should he at the end of it be approved by a committee of officers he will be granted his commission as a sub-lieutenant. While serving his twelve months in the ranks the "candidate" has to perform his share of guards, drills, &c., but instead of living and messing in a common barrack room he will share one with other "candidates," and though drawing no pay during the whole of that time he will be supplied with all the necessary kit, rations, &c., at the government's expense.

The Military College is divided into a number of sections, in each of which special attention is devoted to a certain branch of the service, such as infantry, cavalry, field and fortress artillery, engineering and train, the "officer candidate" joining that section representative of his own particular branch. The "candidate students," as they are then called, are divided into three companies, each under the command of a captain, and each company is divided into six sections with lieutenants in charge. The sections are from twenty-five to thirty strong, and each "candidate student" in it is in his turn head or chief of it, and the extraordinary seriousness and earnestness with which they then perform their duties must be seen to be duly appreciated. While the drill and exercises, &c., taught are in keeping with that branch of the service the "candidate student" aspires to be a member of, all the candidates alike study tactics, topography, military administration, field hygiene, &c., but no foreign language in particular, as is the case with their comrades of the navy. At the close of every year a grand

A CAVALRY LIEUTENANT OF THE IMPERIAL BODYGUARD

graduating ceremony is held, which the Emperor and all his high officers of state make a point of attending

After two years' service as sub-lieutenant the Japanese officer receives his promotion to a lieutenancy, and should lie have shown special keenness and aptitude for his calling he is then sent for a course of study to the Military Staff College. The course there is a three years' one, and a remarkably comprehensive one, too, the officers going through it being attached from time to time to branches of the service other than their own. Those that pass with success receive diplomas and distinctive badges that they wear ever afterwards ; these badges distinguish them most markedly from their brother officers who have not gone through a similar ordeal. From officers trained thus the staff of the Japanese army is recruited; with what happy results has been most signally shown during the late war.

Besides the Staff College each branch of the service in the Japanese army has its own particular school of instruction, and then there is for all of them the Toyama Military College, where officers, non-commissioned officers and men are put through courses of tactics, gymnastics, fencing, musketry, gunnery, &c. But while so much is done for the education and training of the combatant ranks the non-combatants are not forgotten. Military surgeons for instance complete their training at the Army Medical College, and this after graduating from the Medical College, Imperial University. The veterinary surgeons are recruited from graduates of the Agricultural College, Komeba, receiving an after and finishing education at the Army Veterinary School, Tokyo. Military intendants and paymasters are trained at the Military Administration College.

With regard to the training of the rank and file of the

Japanese army and navy, it may here be pointed out, little or no attention is paid by the officers to the teaching of parade and show movements to their men, or to what is so generally and so falsely termed "smartness" among us, and perhaps more especially so is this the case when we come to such matters as relate to the instructions given the recruit in the use of the sword and bayonet. Loose play and plenty of it is invariably their rule, and so, though a squad of Japanese soldiers or sailors may not be able to go through the sword or bayonet exercise with the same precision as a squad of our guardsmen, it will certainly be found that far and away a greater proportion of them will know how to use the weapons they are armed with better and more effectively. Women not occupying the position in Japanese society they do in the West, little or no pains are taken by the military authorities of the Mikado to cater for their amusement, and the result is one never sees any "Agricultural Hall tomfoolery" in Japan.

Having decided, in 1868, upon Westernising the governmental institutions of the empire, the Japanese Government there and then adopted the continental system of universal conscription. What a bold step to take this was may be realised by appreciating the fact that, not only did the *samurai* of those days regard the following of arms as their own peculiar prerogative, but the country, as a result of the abolition of feudalism, was over-run by hordes of these men, whose chances of martial occupation seemed gone for ever. Unfortunately for themselves, however, not only were the lower class *samurai* averse to the bearing and use of Western arms, but they were also so imbued with the clan spirit and jealousies of the time that the gathering together of a number of them in barracks would inevitably have resulted in fights and quarrels innumerable. And so it came about that while the officers and non-commissioned officers of the newly organised national army were recruited solely from the ranks of the better-class *samurai*, the men were mostly recruited from the sturdy farmer and artisan classes of the land; but as the necessity for a larger army arose, as a result of the French, German and Russian interference over the Liaotung Peninsula affair of 1895, merchants and even the much despised actor and other classes were drawn upon to supply the necessary number of recruits for the Mikado's army.

Sent on service for the first time in 1876-77, to suppress the Satsuma rebellion, the newly organised national army did not do quite so well as might have been supposed, but then, it must be remembered, it was called upon to face veteran soldiers of the same race as the men composing it, and, moreover, "veteran soldiers" belonging to the most warlike of all the clans of old Japan, and with all the prestige of a successful revolution behind them, and with much of the sympathy of the nation to encourage them. The result was that as the newly-raised troops had not then learnt either to shoot straight or to use their bayonets aright, the Satsuma swordsmen often proved themselves more than a match for them. Perceiving this, and being fully alive to the necessity for taking prompt measures, the government commenced enlisting a number of the old-time style of Japanese swordsmen, and these with the police, who were all *samurai*, and therefore good swordsmen too, soon. put an end to the revolution and the lives of thousands of their plucky but misguided fellow-countrymen. A few years later, however, the new army did remarkably well in the Formosan affair, and what a good account it gave of itself in China in 1894-95, and again in 1900, is now a matter for history; its recent marvellous doings against the Russians have gained for it the world-renowned fame it so well deserves.

CHAPTER III

"Kenjutsu," or Japanese Fencing

IN few countries has the sword had so much attention and honour paid it as in Japan; for regarded as being of divine origin, it has been worshipped as such. In the interests of veracity it must further be admitted that few swordsmen in other lands have, from a European standpoint, so defiled their blades as those of Japan. For instance, it was quite a common occurrence, even so lately as the seventies of the last century, for a *samurai*, or gentleman soldier of old Japan, to pay a small fee to the public executioner for the privilege of being allowed to test his blade upon the carcase of a criminal, and even at times upon the living body of one. And some Japanese swordsmen, with the same object in view, went further than this, and hesitated not to resort to what they so expressively termed "crossroad-cutting," the victim in such a case being generally a beggar-man, woman, or child, it mattered not which to them.

The very old-time Japanese sword, the *tsurugi*, was a very different sort of weapon to what one now sees in museums and on sale at curio shops in England. It had a straight, double-edged blade, some three feet or more in length, and was not so unlike the sword of the Western knight of old. The *katana*, the medieval and modern sword of Japan, is a much lighter and shorter weapon, with a single-edged blade

32

"KENJUTSU," OR JAPANESE FENCING

slightly curving toward the point. Worn with the *katana*, but by *samurai* alone, was the *wakizashi*, a dirk with a blade of from eight to twelve inches in length, and it was with this that the *harakiri*, or "happy dispatch," as it has been termed, was performed.

Curiously enough the word *harakiri*, though made up from two Japanese words, *hara*, or belly and *kiri* or cutting, is of European invention. No Japanese, except in joke and at the expense of the foreigner, ever thinks of using the term, always preferring the synonym *seppuku*. There were two kinds of seppuku, obligatory and voluntary, and as Professor Chamberlain says, in his "Things Japanese" with respect to this subject:- "The former was a boon granted by the government, who graciously permitted criminals of the Samurai class to destroy themselves instead of being handed over to the common executioner. Time and place were officially notified to the condemned, and officials were sent to witness the ceremony. This custom is quite extinct. Voluntary *hara-kiri* was practised by men in hopeless trouble, also out of loyalty to a dead superior." And then the Professor goes on to give some well-known examples of this last:-

"Examples of this class still take place ; one was mentioned in the newspapers of April of this very year, 1901, and two others in May. That of a young man called Ohara Takeyoshi, which occurred in 1891, is typical. He was a lieutenant in the Yezo militia, and ripped himself up in front of the graves of his ancestors at the temple of Saitokuji in Tokyo. Following the usual routine in such cases, Lieutenant Ohara left a paper setting forth the motives of his act, the only innovation being that this document was directed to be

33

forwarded to the Tokyo News Agency for publication in all the newpapers. The writer, it seems, had brooded for eleven years over the likelihood of Russian encroachment in the northern portion of the Japanese empire, and feeling that his living words and efforts were doomed to fruitlessness, resolved to try what his death might effect. In this particular instance no result was obtained.

Nevertheless, Ohara's self-sacrifice, its origin in political considerations, and the expectation that an appeal from the grave would move men's hearts more surely than any arguments urged by a living voice - all this was in complete accord with Japanese ways of thinking. The government had no sooner yielded to the demands of France, Russia, and Germany, by giving up the conquered province of Liaotung, than forty military men committed suicide in the ancient way.

Even women are found ready to kill themselves for loyalty and duty, but the approved method in their case is cutting the throat. Nowise strange, but admirable to Japanese ideas, was it that when, in 1895, the news of Lieutenant Asada's death on the battlefield was brought to his young wife, she at once, and with her father's consent, resolved to follow him. Having thoroughly cleansed the house and arrayed herself in her costliest robes, she placed her husband's portrait in the alcove, and prostrating herself before it, cut her throat with a dagger that had been a wedding gift."

Just what gave rise to the custom of seppuku it is difficult to say, but it probably had its origin in the desire of vanquished warriors to avoid the humiliations of falling into their enemies' hands alive. This was, undoubtedly, the case in the many instances one heard of at the commencement of

"KENJUTSU," OR JAPANESE FENCING

the late war in the Far East, when Japanese officers and men committed seppuku by hundreds to escape being made prisoners of war by the Russians. The young *samurai* of old, besides learning how to use his weapons aright, was also taught how to perform *seppuku* in the approved fashion, which was as follows:

A SAMURAI ABOUT TO PERFORM SEPPUKU

Having bathed and taken leave of his friends, the would-be suicide then spread a rug or sheet or something of the sort on the matted floor of his room, and sitting down in front of the alcove, facing his family tablets, he then unclothed the upper portion of his body - down to the waist. Tucking the disengaged garments under and behind his thighs, he then took his *wakizashi,* and unsheathing it, pressed the blade to his forehead while he bowed forward, and toward the tablets. Then grasping the dirk by the right hand he plunged the blade deeply into his belly, and with the assistance of the left hand, helped to draw it across it. The disengaged garments tucked under his thighs prevented his falling backwards when he could no longer sit upright through pain and weakness, that being considered anything but a proper way for a *samurai* to fall. The women's *seppuku* was carried out more by a stab in the throat than a direct, cutting of it, and in their case their garments were so fastened around by a cord as to minimise all chances of the same becoming disarranged during their final death struggles.

"Cherished by the *samurai* as almost part of his own self, and considered by the common people as their protector against violence, what wonder," says Mr. McClatchie, "that we should find it [the sword] spoken of in glowing terms by Japanese writers as 'the precious possession of lord and vassal from time older than the divine period,' or as 'the living soul of the *samurai*'?" And again, what wonder that the Japanese should have many a good sword story to tell. One told me by my old fencing master is not only interesting and amusing, but also thoroughly illustrative of the grim humour of the *samurai* with regard to the testing of sword blades, and is as follows:

According to him, there lived in days gone by a certain *daimyo*, or feudal lord, who was a great patron of swordsmiths and swordsmen. One day a swordsmith in his service presented him with a beautiful blade he had but just lately finished. Desirous of seeing it tested the *daimyo* sent for the crack swordsman among his retainers, and upon his arrival ordered him to test the blade upon the body of a fish hawker who chanced to be passing along a road lying within the precincts of the castle. Putting the sword in his girdle in the

place of his own, which he left behind him in the charge of
a friend, the great swordsman strutted off down the road,

A SAMURAI IN CEREMONIAL COSTUME

met and passed the fish-hawker, and then returned to

his feudal lord by another and shorter road. Furious with him the *daimyo* asked why he had not carried out the instructions given him? Begging his lord to have patience, the swordsman asked him to watch the fish-hawker carefully when he came to a certain sharp turning in the road. This he did, and to his wondering surprise saw him collapse all of a sudden, for while the upper portion of his body toppled over one way the lower half fell another. The moral attached to the story is, of course, that not only was the sword an unusually fine one, but the swordsman who wielded it so dexterous, and with so true an edge had he made his cut, that it only required the twisting swing of the fish-baskets to finish his job.

Up to 1876 all *samurai* wore two swords, that being their particular mark of distinction, and the different ways of carrying the weapon indicated the rank of the wearer. Men of high birth wore theirs with the hilt pointing straight upwards; the common people, who were only allowed to wear one sword, and then too, only when on a journey, wore theirs stuck horizontally in the obi, or girdle-like sash of the Japanese; while ordinary *samurai* wore theirs in a position about halfway between the other two. To clash the sheath of one's sword against the hilt belonging to another person was held to be a grave breach of etiquette; to turn the sheath in the belt, as though about to draw, was tantamount to a challenge; while to lay one's weapon on the door of a room, and to kick the guard with the foot in the direction of anyone else, was a deadly insult that generally resulted in a combat to the death. It was not even thought polite to draw a sword from its sheath without begging the permission of

"KENJUTSU," OR JAPANESE FENCING

any other person present. A Japanese gentleman of the old school calling on another, even though he might be his most intimate friend, invariably left his sword with the door keeper of the house, so little did such men, apparently, trust each other.

ILL-TIMED POINT AND RESULT

As I believe that I was the first Occidental to make a study of Japanese swordsmanship, it may be of interest if I here describe my experiences in the fencing schools of Tokyo; and so to begin: the summer of 1888 found me established in Tokyo, and as the sedentary nature of my duties commenced to tell on my health, I decided to take up the study of *kenjutsu*, or Japanese fencing. Getting into touch with the authorities at the Keishicho, or head police station of Tokyo, I soon secured an introduction

39

to Umezawa-san, the fencing master of the Takanawa Police
Station, and then quite one of the best swordsmen in Japan.

THE AUTHOR AND UMEZAWA-SAN

Never did a *maitre d'armes* take more interest and pride
in a pupil than Umezawa did in me, and this was all the
more commendable on his part, because the majority of
the fencing masters in Tokyo looked upon his teaching
me Japanese swordsmanship as a sort of renegade act. The

40

first dozen lessons or so were given me on the little lawn in front of my house, but after a while I used to attend daily at the Takanawa fencing room, and for

A SIDE-SLIP, AND WHAT WOULD HAPPEN

a couple of months or so fenced with, or rather took instructions from, the best fencers attending there. When he thought I was sufficiently advanced Umezawa set me to fence with some of the more indifferent and harder hitting swordsmen, but was always close at hand to give instructions and to correct

41

faults. Writing as an old cavalry man, with plenty of experience of regimental drill grounds and gymnasiums, I can safely say that the Japanese system of teaching swordsmanship is far and away superior to the absurd sword exercise system in vogue in the British army, and that for rough dismounted work the Japanese system of two-handed swordsmanship is much superior to any of the systems of Europe. A first-class French or Italian duellist would, more than probably, beat a first-class Japanese swordsman, but only so if fighting on ground thoroughly suitable to his own peculiar style of sword-play. On rough ground, on a hill side, or on ground covered with impedimenta, the Japanese swordsman would more than likely have the advantage; or in other words, in positions where a rough-and-tumble fight is going on, and where men want to kill, and kill quickly, without attending too much to details of form over it.

As a weapon of offence and defence a *katana* is an infinitely superior one to the ridiculous, single-handed sword with its 36-inch blade, with which British infantry officers are armed, and with slight modifications in its make and use the katana could be rendered still more effective. In the first place, its blade is considerably shorter - from ten to fifteen inches-thus allowing for the majority of men greater freedom of movement; for nobody can deny that to a dismounted man a long scabbard is a horrible nuisance, and that to a short-ishly-inclined man it is an absolute incumbrance. But though shorter in the blade the *katana* has a longer grip, and when one has learnt to use it aright it is truly wonderful what little length of reach is lost. This great length of grip permits of the use of both hands for the purpose of delivering a crushing blow or cut; and, moreover, after practising the Japanese style of fencing, a swordsman becomes quite ambidextrous. How very disconcerting this last is to an opponent all swordsmen are fully aware, and when to this is added the fact that *katana* play is a closer play than that of the cut-and-thrust sword of the Occident, it must be admitted that it is an infinitely superior one to it for the one and great purpose of a fight to the death. It certainly is not so taking to the eye as - let us say - a French or Ital-

Lately, you became greatly disciplined in fencing. I admire you very much

I. ONODA

ian swordsman's play; but while there is less ostentatious art and ceremony about it, there certainly is just as much science, and it may also be added as much, if not more, deadly intent.

Among the many swordsmen who used to put in their daily attendance at the Takanawa fencing-room was one who very early attracted my attention. He was an elderly man, and in some respects a finer swordsman than Umezawa, who introduced him to me one day as his *sensei* or teacher. Onoda was his name, and though he was exceedingly tall for a

Japanese he was quite the best built one I have come across. For a long time I could gather nothing more about him than that he did not like foreigners, and that it would be just as well if I did not thrust my acquaintanceship upon him.

Later on I learnt that he was, or had been, the hereditary fencing master to the late Shogun or "generalissimo" of Japan. All this, of course, helped to arouse my curiosity, but a grimmer or more forbidding-looking old man never lived than Onoda *sensei*; and so what was my surprise when, some six months after I had begun learning *kenjutsu*, he came up to me one afternoon and, presenting his card, offered to take me on for a bout. Delighted at the thought, I was soon ready, but no sooner did the other fencers in the room see what was going to happen than they stopped fencing; and, making quite a ring round us, stood looking on with what I could not help thinking were quite troubled faces. They knew well that Onoda-san had highly disapproved of my being admitted to the fencing-room, and I am not sure but that some of them did not think my days were about to be numbered.

They were quite wrong, and Onoda-san and myself got on so well after this, that, instead of keeping aloof from me any longer, he rather sought me out than otherwise for my company. In his way, he was a most peculiar old fellow, a sort of Buddhist puritan, and when he found out I had spent some years in India he was forever asking me questions about it, its people and their religions, etc. He did a thing one day I never knew another adult Japanese to do, (though I have known one or two of my very young friends among them do a similar thing), and that was to reprove a fellow-countryman of his for being rude to me and calling out

after me in the streets.being an old *samurai*, with an excep-
tionally fine presence and manner, he did this in a way that
sent that erring individual literally grovelling in the dust of
the road. With such a man as my friend and instructor, I soon

MEMBERS OF THE TAKANAWA FENCING SCHOOL

was more than able to hold my own with the average good
swordsmen of Tokyo, and remarkably useful I found the
power of being able to do so, for it brought me into contact
with a class of Japanese that few, if any other foreigners have
ever had the chance of becoming acquainted with. However,
to revert to the *kenjutsu*.

45

The *kabuto*, or helmet, is in many respects superior to the mask worn by the sabre-players of Europe, but while it gives ample protection to the face, neck, and throat, it does not sufficiently protect the sides of the head, nor yet its top or crown. It sits much firmer, however, than do any of our fencing helmets or masks, being tied, or rather lashed, on to the head. Under it is invariably worn a *tenugui*, or small native towel, wrapped round the head in turban-like fashion, as shown in the photograph, in which I am seen standing by the side of Umezawa-san. The reason for this is of a purely cleanly or sanitary nature, and the result is that no Japanese helmets ever have an unpleasant odour.

The *do*, or corselet, is a lighter, cooler, and in every way a far superior chest and body protector to the leather jerkins of European sabre-players. It is made of slips of the very best and soundest of bamboos, strung perpendicularly together in the required shape, and trimmed and strengthened with fastenings of leather, silk, or hemp. The best *do* are lacquered with the *mon* or crest of the owner, and remarkably handsome some of them are. They are worn hanging some what loosely, being suspended from the shoulders by soft cords of cotton or silk, but never so loosely as to prove a nuisance to the swordsman.

The *kusadzuri*, or taces, is a light and efficient enough protector for the lower part of the body, but hardly as good as those in use in British gymnasiums. These are generally made of a tough cotton or hempen canvas, cut in five strips of about nine inches in length and four in width, two strips lying under, and three outside. Each of the strips is quilted, and bound round the edges with leather. Though hanging loose the strips are fastened to a band that encircles the waist of the fencer, but in a way that does not impede his movements in the slightest degree.

The *kote*, or gauntlet, is a hand, wrist, and forearm guard, much superior, in many respects, to anything of the sort to

PRIOR TO THE SALUTE

be seen in our gymnasiums. A *kote* is made of strong cotton or hempen canvas, lined with bamboo shavings or horse-hair, and trimmed and strengthened with a soft, kidlike leather. One great advantage the Japanese *kote* possesses over our gauntlets is that its size can be regulated up to quite an appreciable degree by the loosening or tightening of the lacing running along and inside its forearm portion. The *shinai*, or practice sword, is made from four strips of bamboo, and though it undoubtedly looks clumsy enough at first, it is not so by any means. The length and weight of *shinai* vary according to the taste of fencers, there being no rule laid down about this - surely a fairer method than ours, which forces all men to use the same-sized practice sword, irrespective of their stature and strength. The four strips of bamboo being cut to fit each other are then brought together, and over the grip or handle end of the *shinai* is drawn a strong leather covering. The grip may be of any length, say from eight to sixteen inches, or more. From the guard end of this covering runs a leather or gut strand to the point of the *shinai*, and is there fastened to a leather cup-like covering that keeps together the ends of the four bamboos, and forms a button over their points. The line along which the gut runs is considered the back of the sword, and as the *shinai* is strengthened and kept together by a fastening of leather at its cutting point, advantage is taken of this to run the gut through it, and so help to keep it all the tauter in its place. The tsuba, or guard, is a circular piece of stout leather, with a hole in its centre to permit of its being passed up and over the grip until it reaches the hilt, where it forms a circular guard, standing out from the *shinai* an inch, or a little more. Sometimes, but not often, a fencer will use a secondary tsuba, made of thin leather and padded like a cushion. This will lie between his hand and the ordinary tsuba. The measurements of my favourite *shinai* are: blade, twenty-six inches, and grip fourteen inches. But it must be pointed out here that I stand but a trifle over five feet six inches, and have somewhat small hands.

The hakama, or divided skirt of the *samurai*, is a most comfortable article of clothing, which, while it affords a

"KENJUTSU," OR JAPANESE FENCING

certain amount of protection the legs and lower parts of the body, does not in the least impede a fencer's movements. It is light, airy, and cool, and might, with very great advantage, be introduced into England, in a modified form, for the use of young girls.

THE ENGAGE

Japanese fencing-rooms are all built on more or less the same plan, and the Takanawa fencing-room was no exception to this. It was about thirty feet in length and about half that inwidth. Two of its sides were opened to the air, and along its other two sides ran a raised platform, a couple of feet or so above the floor of the fencing arena. The platform was furnished with mats, and on cold days with fire-boxes, and was used indiscriminately as galleries for spectators or dressing and resting-rooms for the fencers. Such men as liked to keep their fencing gear there could do so, hanging the same up on pegs along the side of the gallery. Here it must be pointed out that all Japanese fencers have their own special kit, the fencing-room supplying nothing.

Two men agreeing to have a bout will, after donning their kit, step into the arena, and squatting down in front of each other, at about eight feet apart, will then proceed to salute one another by a bow. Rising slowly they will put themselves into position with *shinai* crossing at engage, as shown in the illustration.

To go into details over all the cuts, guards, and points of a Japanese fencer's *répertoire* is not the object of this article, but it is well to point out here that during fifteen years' experience of *kenjutsu* I remember seeing only one man make use of a real back-handed stroke, and he - though one of the best swordsmen in Japan-took the idea, I fancy, from seeing me use it. Another remarkable point about the Japanese system of swordsmanship is that its votaries never deliver a point except at the throat; but this is, perhaps, to be explained by the fact that until the seventies armour was largely used by them. This point even is more of a job than a lunging thrust, and is delivered from below upwards, with the very evident object of getting in between the gorget and the upper part of the breastplate. Though highly scientific, *kenjutsu* is a very rough-and-tumble sort of sword-play, absolutely free from parade and all theatrical touches, but wonderfully practical withal. As Japanese chivalry is most uncompromisingly based upon the idea that all is fair in war, so Japanese swordsmen resort to certain methods which are highly reprehensible from our point of view. Such a thing as giving another man a chance never appears to enter their heads; and so, should a fencer lose his *shinai*, or fail in any way, his adversary immediately takes advantage of this to push home his attack with all the greater vigour.

CORPS À CORPS À LA JAPONAISE

The cuts most in favour with Japanese swordsmen are mainly of the chopping order, and mostly delivered at the head and right wrist. Some few, however, pay particular attention to their adversary's stomach, and, if skilful swordsmen, these are the most difficult to tackle. The cuts at the head and wrist can be delivered from the engage position, and in the case of the former this is done by slightly raising the *shinai*, stepping sharply forward, and as sharply bringing the *shinai* down upon the adversary's head with a chop that carries on.

The wrist cut is made by a disengaging cut-over, with, if necessary a sharp side tap against the adversary's *shinai* to throw it out of line. Both these cuts can be parried by a slight raising of the *shinai* and an outward twist of the wrist, and from both parries return cuts can be made at either head or wrist. Ordinarily Japanese fencers stand much closer to each other than do those of Europe, and it is truly remarkable what little space a couple of good native swordsmen require for a fight to the death. Some on the contrary are very fond of keeping well away and, if not followed up and brought to close quarters, resort to a widely different mode of attack, consisting mainly of slashing cuts, first with one hand and then with the other, the changes being carried out with wonderful rapidity. The principal swinging cut can be delivered for either side of an opponent's head, but if he is a good swordsman it is a some-what risky one to resort to, for he can reply to it by either a stop thrust or a stop cut at the head. The guard for it is a mere raising of the sword to a sufficient height and in the right line. There is only one form of hanging guard known to Japanese swordsmen, and it is seldom resorted to, for it makes a smart return a matter of great difficulty.

The Japanese inhabiting a mountainous country have from time immemorial accustomed themselves to fight more on foot than on horseback, while our knights of old, being differently situated, never fought on foot except and only when absolutely obliged by circumstances to do so. That the western systems of swordsmanship of the present day are relics of the old knightly days there can be no manner of doubt. The sword then was the weapon of the mounted man, of a one-handed swordsman, and to be of real use to him it was necessary it should be of a goodly length, but while a mounted man can use a fairly heavy sword with considerable effect and advantage, a dismounted man is distinctly handicapped by being armed with such a weapon. Courtly ways succeeding knightly ways, men then took to wearing lighter made swords, but as it was still considered more honourable to fight on horseback than on foot, and as men could not forever be changing their swords, and as a thrusting sword was just as effective under the newer conditions ruling the non-wearing of armour, so the rapier eventually came more and more into use in the West. With the rapier came the great reliance the European swordsman puts on the point, and with it also came the necessity for fighting on strictly straight lines in contradistinction to lines which enable and permit the breaking of ground by a rougher style of swordsmanship. To use the point to the best advantage a lunging thrust is required, and to deliver a lunging thrust aright it is essential that the ground underfoot should be free of impedimenta, and also on a plane. The existence of such conditions cannot, however, be relied upon, and the consequence is the more the sword approaches the rapier in construction the less suitable it is for use on rough ground. Now the *katana* can be used as well on rough as on smooth and level ground, but though a wonderfully effective weapon it is by no means a perfect one, nor is *katana*-play alone - pure and simple - a perfect system of swordsmanship. Such can only be arrived at by making a new style of sword and instituting a new style of sword-play, combining in them all that is best in the swords of the West and the swords of the Far East, and in the methods employed in their use.

Some of the best points about *kenjutsu* are, that from every guard or parry some two or more different returns can be made, and that such guards or parries are more of a fending-off order than strictly stopping ones, thus allowing the returns to be made more quickly and the guards with less exertion. Again, neither strength nor length of each are of such great advantage in *kenjutsu*, as they are in our Western systems of sword-play, and so men of varying sizes and degrees of strength are brought on footings of greater equality when practising it than they would be with us. And then again, while just as scientific as our systems of sword-play, the Japanese system is a much less artificial one, and so with the majority of men less time would be required for picking up a knowledge of it.

Very naturally a good swordsman is held in high repute among the Japanese, but curiously enough a good sword-smith is perhaps more so; and the names of such men as Amakune, Kamige, Shinsoku, and Amaza of the very olden days, and Munechika, Yasutsuna, Sanemori, Yukihira, and Yoshimitsu of the middle ages, are known to all educated subjects of the Mikado; and then as for Masamune, Yoshi-hiro, and Munemasa, their names are household words in every homestead of the land. The two best swordsmen I have met in Japan were Sakakibara and Henmi. The first was a tall, rather slightly built man, but though a grand swordsman, somewhat inclined to play to the gallery. Henmi-san, on the other hand, was a most unobtrusive individual, standing about five-feet-one, and quite the most graceful moving man I have ever seen; but though Sakakibara had a greater following among the general public of Tokyo, there is little doubt Henmi was the better swordsman of the two. I have seen him, while fencing with a first-class swordsman, stop all of a sudden, drop his *shinai*, and then invite the other to attack him. But try as this other might, he could seldom get a cut into him, for where Henmi was the fraction of a second before, the spot would be vacant.

The Japanese have always been very fond of giving names to their swords, such names being usually derived from some circumstance connected with their career. The "Grass-mowing sword" for instance, the most highly prized of all the swords of Japan, was so called because, when a brushwood fire threatened to destroy his army, Yamato Take mowed down the intervening brushwood with it, and so stopped the flames and saved his troops. Yamato Take, it may here be mentioned, was the son of the Emperor Keiko, 71-181 A.D. The "Hige-Kiri" and "Hizamaru" were two famous swords belonging to the Minamoto family, and owe their names to the fact that when they were tested on a couple of criminals sentenced to decapitation, one cut through the *hige* or beard of the victim after severing the head from the body, while the second cut through the *hiza* or knee of the other luckless wretch as he sat or squatted to receive his death blow.

The following among other mottoes are sometimes found engraved on the hilt of Japanese swords:-

"There's nought twixt heaven and earth that man need fear who carries at his belt this single blade."

"One's fate is in the hands of heaven, but a skilful fighter does not meet with death."

"In one's last days one's sword becomes the wealth of one's posterity"

CHAPTER IV

Japanese Wrestling

Sumo and Jujutsu

FEW people are so keen about wrestling as the Japanese, who have for centuries past practised two distinct kinds-*sumo* and *jujutsu*. As regards the difference existing between the two, it is worth noting that this is something more than a mere difference of style as between two schools of the same art. For while the votaries of *sumo* rely as much upon their personal strength and weight of body as upon any knowledge they may possess of scientific grips and falls, those of *jujutsu* aim solely at overthrowing an opponent by highly reasoned-out yieldings of self, or as a Japanese would put it, " by yielding to strength." And then again, while the *sumotori* are essentially professional wrestlers, recruited mainly from the lower strata of Japanese society, among the devotees of *jujutsu*- muster men of birth and education, and often, too, of high social position and standing.

Without going into undue details as regards the history of wrestling in Japan, it may here be as well to point out that until thirty years ago the *sumotori*, ranked next in social matters to the *samurai*, the soldier nobility of old Japan, for it was considered that their profession was a semi-military one. Now, however, all this is changed, and, instead of living lives of ease and honour under the protecting aegis of some

great feudal lord or high dignitary of State, the *sumotori* of
to-day have to content themselves with dangling after the

KAWADSU-NO-SABURO AND MATANO NO-GORO, TWO
CELEBRATED WRESTLERS OF OLD

heels of some one of their country's erstwhile despised *shonin*,
or "merchants." But fortunately for them and the cause of
sumo, the " Wrestlers' Guild " is still well to the fore, and

JAPANESE WRESTLING

not only helps and succours them in trouble and sickness, butexercises over them and their calling a beneficent despotism not unlike that exercised by the Jockey Club over horseracing in England. In days gone by the *sumotori* enjoyed many privileges-such as immunity from bridge and ferry

MIGI-YOTTSU, OR " FOUR GRIPS." RIGHT HANDS INSIDE

tolls, and they could also claim the hire of post-horses at specially low rates. Theatres, booths at fairs, and other places of amusement were policed by them, and without the permission of their guild the managers of such exhibitions dared not open.

The "Wrestlers' Guild" has its headquarters in Tokyo, and the officers in charge of its affairs have always been recruited from the retired list of old wrestlers and umpires. Both *sumotori* and umpires enter upon their calling when

A POSTURING EXERCISE FOR STRENGTHENING
THE THIGH MUSCLES

quite young, and in the generality of cases owe their first start in life to the benevolent influence of some famous wrestler or umpire. Once fairly started upon their career, however, they then come under the orders of the guild, and without the sanction of that august body no wrestler may compete in any tournament or match, with the result that such a thing as "selling a match" is an unknown thing among the *sumotori* of Japan. While the umpires retain their family nomenclature, the wrestlers have professional names bestowed upon them, as, for instance, Taiho, or "Great Gun," Nishi-no-Ume, or "Western Ocean," &c., &c.,--all indicative of great size and strength. For the *sumotori*, it may here be remarked, are all huge men, almost giants in comparison to the ruck of their fellow-countrymen, and yet despite of their great paunches and the lumps and rolls of fat that encase their bodies, they are not only enormously strong, but active withal. Curiously enough, the training of the *sumotori* is in strict opposition to all theories held upon such subjects by English athletes and trainers, for not only do they eat and drink excessively, but also any kind of food or liquor they may fancy. And then, as regards their work outside of the ring, it consists mainly in butting at posts with their shoulders and chests, and in lifting and flinging about and catching weights in the shape of sacks of rice, sand, and the like. They also go through a good deal of posturing with a view to the loosening and suppling of their limbs, and, perhaps, too, as a sort of balancing practice.

A budding aspirant for umpire honours is generally a member of a family that has followed that calling for generations, and commences his study of palaestral matters under the supervision of a thoroughly trustworthy senior. When deemed sufficiently advanced he will be put to umpire practice bouts and the bouts of novices, and he gets his promotion according to vacancies and his own competency.

F.J. NORMAN'S THE FIGHTING MAN OF JAPAN

According to Japanese records, the first great umpire was Shiga Seirin, who umpired the wrestling matches fought out before the Emperor Shonin (724-749 A.D.). The baton of office wielded by an umpire is a fan of the old time military type ; similarly antique is his costume. His orders

A GROUP OF BUDDING ASPIRANTS FOR PALAESTRAL HONOURS, WITH A YOUNG UMPIRE STANDING AMONG THEM

and injunctions to the wrestlers and his address to the spectators are given in a peculiarly high-pitched tone, very dramatically and very penetratingly. Ranking next to a *samurai*, and often one, an umpire is allowed to wear a sword, and at all great matches he invariably does so. According to their skill so the *sumotori* are divided into classes, weight having nothing to do with the matter, and

JAPANESE WRESTLING

the classifying of them is altogether in the hands of the guild. Their examinations for class honours are carried out twice a year, in January and May, within the famous temple grounds of Ekoin, in Tokyo, and excites immense enthusiasm among all classes of that great city's population. For days before the contest the streets are made noisier than

TACHI-AI, OR "WATCHING FOR AN OPENING"

usual by men beating drums, announcing the day and flour upon which the matches are to commence, and, besides all this, a great drumming is kept up on a specially prepared tower called a Yagura, standing some forty feet high and immediately in front of the wrestling booth. An amphitheatre having been erected, in the centre of it is left a square arena, and in the centre of this again is built up an eighteen feet square structure to a height of from two to four feet above the level of the ground. This is unrailed, though roofed over, the pillars supporting the roof being firmly planted at the four corners, and in the exact centre of all is pitched the wrestling ring, twelve feet in diameter, marked out by a plaited straw rope. The pillars and roof are adorned with draperies, flags, bannerets, &c., and the whole turn-out makes quite a, brave show.

When all is ready *a toshiyori*, or elder from among the retired wrestlers, steps into the arena and declares the meeting opened, and the *sumotori*, who are divided into two parties, then file into it from opposite sides. One party is invariably called the east and the other the west, and when they have finished filing in they squat down, the members of each party on their own side of the arena. Two of the least skilful of the contestants then step into the ring, one from each side, being ushered in by a junior umpire, who, after introducing them to the spectators by their professional names and status, orders them to commence. Being low down the grade of wrestlers, they, as also the half-a-dozen or so couples that follow immediately after, dispense with preliminaries, as much, perhaps, because of their ignorance of them as for any more valid reason. Not so, however, their seniors, who, after having been ushered into the ring and introduced to the spectators by an umpire of an equal status to themselves, proceed to go through some of the most fantastic and extraordinary posturings and preliminaries imaginable, winding up by taking a pinch of salt and tossing the same in the air as an oblation to Nomi-no Sukune, the tutelary deity of the wrestlers of Japan.

JAPANESE WRESTLING

A mawashi, or "loin cloth," is all that covers a *sumotori's* nakedness while actually engaged in a bout. It is generally made of hemp, but sometimes of silk, and may be either white or red in colour. The aprons worn during posturing

DŌ·HYO·IRI OR "CEREMONIAL APRON," AS WORN BY
FIRST-CLASS JAPANESE WRESTLERS

and preliminaries by the highest ranked *sumotori* are the Japanese equivalents of a British pugilist's belt, and being richly embroidered in gold and silk sometimes cost as much as 1,000 yen, equal to about £100. *Sumotori* invariably allow their hair to grow as long as possible, shaving off, however, a portion of it in front, and tying it back into a queue, fasten it on the top and back of their heads.

When both wrestlers have done with their preliminaries they take up their positions within and on opposite sides is a very short-lived affair indeed, seldom lasting over a minute, and the reason is that the men are as often as not

SIKI-KABURI. A BACK. THROW FOILED

afraid to grapple for fear of being pushed, butted, or thrown out of the ring. Squatting on their haunches they watch for an opening, and when one of them sees it he immediately makes a dart at the other, but the chances are his opponent will not recognise it as a fair start. This may occur over and over again, but once fairly started a Japanese wrestling bout

JAPANESE WRESTLING

out of the ring before they have well commenced. For, as has been already pointed out, the ring is but twelve feet in diameter, and the least possible throw, step or push outside of it loses a *sumotori* his bout and perhaps his rank and status

A GROUP OF FAMOUS WRESTLERS, INCLUDING EX-CHAMPION
AND PRESENT CHAMPION OF JAPAN

also, and this means money to him, for according to their rank and status so the men are paid.

There are forty-eight recognised methods or hands for coping with an antagonist, and the Japanese claim they have remained unchanged for centuries. In addition to these, there are a hundred and sixty-eight possible or subsidiary hands. The orthodox hands are classified into throwing, grappling, twisting and bending, each having twelve hands, but these do not, of course, exhaust a good wrestler's resources, which, within certain bounds, depend upon his quickness of eye and decision. Should a wrestler employ methods dangerous to life and limb he is at once admonished, and should he do so again he is promptly ejected from out the arena and the guild, and this is a punishment that carries with it penalties similar in all respects to the suspension of a jockey by the Jockey Club of England.

In the first rank of the *sumotori* stand the Ozeki, then the Sekiwaki and Komusubi. Following them come seven gradations or classes of Mayegashira. Should an Ozeki- prove himself superior to all his rivals of the same rank he is promoted to Hinoshita Kaizan, carrying with it the privilege of wearing the *yokozuka,* or "side rope," a belt in the form of a rope. According to Japanese accounts Akashi Shigenosuke was the first to have this honour conferred upon him, in 1624 A.D., and since his time there have been only sixteen *kaizan,* the latest being Hitachiyama, the present champion of Japan.

Jujutsu

As before explained, *jujutsu* is a very different art to *sumo,* ranking considerably higher than it in the esteem of the more aristocratic portions of Japanese society. Its principles,

68

JAPANESE WRESTLING

like so many other things Japanese, were until lately handed
down as a sort of esoteric secret from one great master of the
art to another, and, unlike as in the case of *sumo*, there are
many schools or styles of *jujutsu*. It is essentially a military
art, and in the feudal days instructions in it formed a no
mean part in the education of a young *samurai*. For some

KO-MATA-DORI. OR "LEG-PULL THROW"

time after the abolition of the feudal system it looked as if
it was going to become one of the many lost arts, but happily
for the future prospects of Japanese manhood a revival took
place, and at present it is extremely popular among all classes
of the Mikado's subjects. Jujutsu is known to the Japanese
under various names, such as *judo, yawara, taijutsu, kogusoku,
kempo* and *hakuda*, but *judo, jujutsu* and *yawara* are the

terms most commonly used. Considering the high esteem in which it has always been held, it is really wonderful what few books there are upon it, and still more wonderful that such as there are have not dealt as fully with it as they might have. Such books, or rather pamphlets, as have dealt with it have generally so done from the particular standpoint of some one of the many schools of *jujutsu,* and there is absolutely no

KATA-SUKASHI, A SIDESLIP FOLLOWED BY A NECK-GRIP THROW

doubt the originators of certain new schools have made history to suit their own purpose. Still, there seems little doubt that, while *kogusoku* and *kempo* were originally two distinct arts, the former the art of *seizing* and the latter the art of *gaining victory by pliancy,* the two were afterwards

70

JAPANESE WRESTLING

amalgamated and formed into one art and that *jujutsu* as we now know it. As to the date when *jujutsu* first became firmly established as an art necessary to the proper training of a warrior, that would appear to have been somewhere about the middle of the seventeenth century. A Chinese refugee named Chingempin had apparently something to do with its introduction into Japan, for his name appears in nearly every

SETTING-TO

pamphlet bearing upon the subject from a historical point of view. But for all that the art, like so many others originally borrowed from the Chinese, is now essentially Japanese.

To explain straight off what *jujutsu* is would indeed puzzle any one, for it stands in somewhat the same category toward

wrestling as fencing does toward single-stick practice, and it
is again an art of fighting without weapons on lines entirely
distinct from those followed by the pugilists of England and

TAI-OTOSHI, OR "STANDING SIDE-THROW"

America, or by the *savate* players of France. An expert at
jujutsu has, figuratively speaking, many cards up his sleeve,
he can throw an opponent heavily enough to daze, to stun
or to kill him ; he can choke, strangle or throttle him with his

JAPANESE WRESTLING

bare hands, arms, legs, or even by twisting his clothing tightly around his neck; he can hold him down on the ground, or in such a position as to render him absolutely helpless, or he can twist and bend his arms, legs or fingers so as to force him to give in through sheer pain.

The different schools of *jujutsu* practise all these various methods of overcoming an opponent, but it is only in sonic of them, that *atemi* and *kuatsu* are taught. *Atemi* is the art of striking, or kicking some particular part of an opponent's body in order to kill, injure, or incapacitate him from further resistance. *Kuatsu*, which means to "resuscitate," is taught only to a favoured few for the purpose of resuscitating those who have apparently died through violence. The methods employed by the practisers of *kuatsu* are many and differ considerably according to the schools, but the one most commonly employed when a man has been stunned by, a fall or blow is to embrace the patient firmly from behind and just under the armpits, to then lift him up to a standing position and to raise him up and down sharply once or twice, allowing his feet to strike the ground each time, and it is truly remarkable how very often and how very efficacious this generally is.

In days gone by the *samurai* learnt *jujutsu* with the same spirit and object in view as they learnt to use a sword, but of late it has been developed into a system of athletics and mental and moral training, and as such it undoubtedly is of inestimable value to the youths of Japan. In the best equipped schools in Tokyo daily instructions are carried out by means of lectures on the theory of the art as well as by actual practice; and, as the best teachers of it so justly claim,

F.J. NORMAN'S THE FIGHTING MAN OF JAPAN

a knowledge of it gives confidence to men and helps them to
face dangers and difficulties in a proper and manly spirit, and
in illustration of this they tell many amusing and instructive

HIKI-OTOSHI, OR "PULL-DOWN THROW"

stories. That of Terada Goyemon must here suffice : Terada
lived in Tokyo some forty years ago, in days when it was
considered necessary for princes and high officers of state to
be accompanied by bands of armed retainers whenever they

74

JAPANESE WRESTLING

showed themselves in public. Being out one day on some
business, Terada fell in with the procession of the Prince
of Mite, and the *sakibarai,* or attendants of the Prince,
while making way for the procession ordered hire to kneel
down, which he refused to do, explaining that a *samurai* of
his rank did not require to kneel unless the Prince's kayo,
or "sedanchair," came nearer. The *sakibarai,* however,
persisted in their endeavours to force him to kneel, and
five or six of them attempted to throw him down, but he
freed himself and threw them all to the ground. Other
sakibarai coming up threatened to kill him, but he threw
them down too, and seizing their *jittei,* small iron rods or
maces, ran over to the Prince's *yashiki,* or official residence,
saying : "I am a *samurai* of such and such a rank, and it is
against the dignity of my feudal lord that I should kneel
down. I regret that I had to throw your men down, but I
had to do it to preserve my honour, and here are the *jittei*
which I return to you." To the credit of the Prince be it
said, he was so pleased with Terada that he asked him to
enter his service. This, however, that true *samurai* refused
to do, claiming that his place was by his own Prince's side.

As regards the present mania in England for *jujutsu* - and
may it increase and live long - it is just as well to point out
here that though the art is undoubtedly a most scientific one,
yet if people will only think for a moment they will realise
how very absurd and sensational are some of the claims
advanced upon its behalf. Time and again I have been asked
how a good *jujutsu* man would shape in front of a first-class
boxer, and the only answer I have ever been able to give is
that it would depend entirely upon the individual exponents

of their own peculiar art. There is no neater fighter in existence than a good boxer, and if such a one got home with his blow first he would most probably knock his man

KEKAESHI, OR ' KICK-BACK THROW

down, if not out ; but if he bungled over the affair in the slightest degree the *jujutsu* man would, or should, be in to him at once, and then there can be little doubt the result would be all in his favour. But when talking of *jujutsu* and

JAPANESE WRESTLING

boxing, comparing the one with the other, people either forget or are unaware that while the majority of Japanese make a perfect study of their own peculiar art, few Englishmen do so of theirs. The result is that skilled *jujutsu* men exist in far greater numbers among the Japanese than skilled boxers do among Englishmen. And then again, to be thoroughly sure of knocking out his man cleanly and efficiently, a boxer must be up to professional form, while a *jujutsu* man, on the other hand, and one, moreover, who need by no means be any great expert, can easily throw and incapacitate any man, except, and only, another and superior exponent of his art. As an auxiliary to fisticuffs and swordplay *jujutsu* certainly ranks high ; that is to say, if one regards and practices those two grand arts from a practical standpoint--as arts of offence and defence rather than of mere physical exercise.

As a physical exercise, pure and simple, there is, however, much to be said in favour of *jujutsu*, for victory does not depend upon a mere question of avoirdupois and brute force, as must be admitted to be the case with the majority of our native arts of offence and self-defence. In fact, the art of *jujutsu is* more mental than muscular, and might well be described as the mathematics of all physical exercises, on such wonderfully exact lines is it based. Balance being the key-note of *jujutsu*, the result of its teachings is a wellbalanced and graceful carriage of the body when standing and when walking, and, it may also be added, when falling, and when getting up from a fall, for how to fall properly is the first thing taught an aspirant for *jujutsu* honours. The result of such teachings is that a student of the art, whether man, woman, or child, soon gains so perfect a control over his or her muscular system as to help minimise, to a wonderful

MISS ROBERTS, LADY INSTRUCTRESS, THE JAPANESE SCHOOL
OF JUJUTSU, APPLYING THE "ARM-BREAK LOCK"

extent, dangers from accidents which might otherwise prove serious, if not fatal ; such, for instance, as so often occur at crossings in the more crowded streets of London; and all this is gained without any undue hardening and mis-shaping of the muscles.

In conclusion, it may be as well here to point out that it is by no means necessary for an intending student of *jujutsu* to be an athlete, rather the other way ; for such athletes, unfortunately, when commencing a course of *jujutsu,* are inclined to rely overmuch on their strength and activity, a fatal mistake if one hopes to attain to any degree of proficiency in the art. Unlike those muscle-trying exercises which necessitate the use of developers, dumb-bells, barbells, &c. (from the sale of which such enormous profits are derived by the proprietors of certain much-vaulted and advertised schools of physical culture), *jujutsu* is a natural art, an unartificial exercise, and one which, partly by reason of its superiority to all extraneous appliances, affords the very healthiest fun, emulation, and exercise in existence.

THE END

A JU-JITSU BOOK.

JUJITSU has suffered from its exploitation by a literature of a somewhat low type. There has been spread abroad a false idea of its nature and of the reasons which justify and make valuable its introduction among the games and sports of England.

It has become desirable, therefore, that a Ju-Jitsu book with some claims to common sense should be obtainable, and the School is therefore preparing a carefully written and carefully illustrated elementary work on the subject. This will be no collection of cut-and-dried recipes, the perusal of which will enable sedentary persons to encounter and overcome large and violent men armed with knives. It will endeavour to outline Ju-Jitsu, the game. It will be the daily teaching of the School put on paper. It will be a book that, in places where no instruction in Ju-Jitsu can be obtained, may be studied together by two or three people, and from it they will he able to extract material for much sport and contest and healthy exercise.

Details as to price and date of publication will be sent to enquirers.

THE JAPANESE SCHOOL OF JU-JITSU,

305, OXFORD STREET, W.

80

www.ingramcontent.com/pod-product-compliance
Lightning Source LLC
Chambersburg PA
CBHW060330050426
42449CB00011B/2715